Also available from Dale Carnegie Training

The 5 Essential People Skills

LEADERSHIP MASTERY

How to Challenge Yourself
and Others to Greatness

DALE CARNEGIE TRAINING

A FIRESIDE BOOK
Published by Simon & Schuster
New York   London   Toronto   Sydney

Fireside
A Division of Simon & Schuster, Inc.
1230 Avenue of the Americas
New York, NY 10020

First Fireside trade paperback edition November 2009

FIRESIDE and colophon are registered trademarks of Simon & Schuster, Inc.

For information about special discounts for bulk purchases, please contact
Simon & Schuster Special Sales at 1-800-456-6798 or
business@simonandschuster.com.

Manufactured in the United States of America

10   9   8   7   6   5   4   3   2

Library of Congress Cataloging-in-Publication Data
   Leadership mastery : how to challenge yourself and others to greatness /
Dale Carnegie Training.
           p.   cm.
      "A Fireside book."
   1. Leadership. 2. Executive ability. I. Dale Carnegie Training (Firm). II. Title.
   HD57.7 .L43434 2009
   658.4'092—dc22
   2009014059

ISBN 978-1-4165-9549-6
ISBN 978-1-4391-3477-1 (ebook)

Originally published as *Dale Carnegie Leadership Mastery Course*
as an audio edition in 2000.

Contents

Preface

Where have all the leaders gone? There is a vacuum of leadership in the world, in all of our major institutions: government, education, business, religion, and the arts. The crisis has arisen in part because many of those institutions have been reinvented. Life is therefore much more uncertain and leadership is hence much more risky. However, most of the leadership crisis has crept up on us because of the incredible technological revolution we're now experiencing. We are told that the scientific method can solve all our problems and that technology can distribute the answers to those problems far more quickly and efficiently than before. A global society connected by the Internet is emerging, yet never have so many people felt so isolated from one another. Individuals the world over find themselves disconnected from their roots and unsure of their future. This is because in a world quickly becoming more virtual, the skill of human relations is quickly being lost. Thus, never before has the skill of human relations been more valuable and sought after.

Just about everyone who is anyone has a Web site and an e-mail address. The only way to differentiate yourself and your business is to become exceptionally skilled at leading and persuading others. Think of it: In the previous era of hierarchical organizations, big government, and traditional families, the need for leadership was evident. We knew what the rules were. We needed the leaders to hold us to those rules. However, in an era of flattened organizations, the increasing irrelevance of government, and two-career families, we no longer have a clear set of rules to follow.

What's more, the command-and-control leaders who try to hold us to seemingly irrelevant and arbitrary rules are no longer successful. What's needed is a new type of leader, one who can inspire and motivate others within this virtual world while never losing sight of the leadership principles that never change. Therefore in this cutting-edge book, we'll introduce you to a new type of leader: a leader who is flexible and adaptable. We'll introduce you to an individual who is a servant, not a slave, to his or her partners; a distributor of power, trustworthy, tough, and decisive.

The core philosophy of this book will be taken from the man whose name has become synonymous with influence and human relations, Dale Carnegie.

In the words of Dale Carnegie himself:

And now I've just got time to tell you about a couple of simple tests that you can make to prove to yourself how easy it is to make people like you instantly; here they are. Test one, starting tomorrow morning, you smile at the first five people you see at work every day for a week. I mean a good, broad, genuine smile and a hearty good morning. Test two, pick out just one person every day for a week, one person who has never meant very much to you, and become genuinely interested in him and show that you're interested in him with a smile and some friendly comment. Now two words of warning; be sincere, utterly and eternally sincere. You will just be wasting your time if you pretend to be interested in other people in order to get something out of them. That's foolish as well as wrong, because you'll be found out sooner or later. Why not make those two simple tests yourself and keep a record of the results. Remember if you want to be liked instantly, do as the puppy does: Become genuinely interested in other people and show it.

These human relations principles have made Dale Carnegie a household name for more than fifty years. Throughout this book, you'll read Dale Carnegie's famous leadership principles exactly as he wrote about them in some of his classic works. Principles like these will never change. It is how they are applied that will change. In the past, an order from the boss may have given the employee enough want. Today leaders must create that want by engaging others in the mission with same the goals but by different processes.

What's more, you'll learn how the virtual world does not have to become more impersonal. You can use high-tech tools to stay in touch as a leader. Yes, leadership, like any other skill, is not something you are born with. It must be learned. When you have read this book and completed all of the action steps at the end of each chapter, you will possess the most vital skill for succeeding in the new economy: the skill of leadership. The need for this skill will only grow in value as our virtual world expands.

Finally, once you have completed this book you'll no longer ask, "Where have all the leaders gone?" You'll realize that leadership is no longer for the chief executive officer, the president, the general, the boss, or the mom and dad. Leadership is available to each and every one of us at every level of organization, be that society, business, government, or family. Complete this book and discover your full potential. Become a leadership master.

Keep your mind open to change all the time. Welcome it. Court it.

—Dale Carnegie

CHAPTER 1

What Leaders Do

In the chapters that follow we'll be engaged in a very ambitious and extremely important undertaking. It will be of great benefit to you, and also to everyone who comes into your life both personally and professionally.

We'll be exploring a fundamental principle of human behavior. It's the basis of successful companies and even of whole nations and cultures. This is the concept of *leadership*. More specifically, we'll focus on the meaning of leadership in the context of business and entrepreneurial success. We'll see how leaders made the most of prosperous times, and how they survived even severe downturns in the business cycle.

Who are the leaders? What are the leaders made of? Who are the men and women who "made it happen" for themselves and the people around them? How did they overcome obstacles? Where did they discover opportunities? This is critically important information for anyone who aspires to financial success, personal satisfaction, and the sense of accomplishment that comes when potential turns into actuality.

In today's world, the quality of leadership is both respected and revered, but it's also subtly devalued. We celebrate the birthdays of Washington and Lincoln, great leaders of the past, yet we are deeply suspicious of those who occupy leadership positions in the present day. Perhaps it's because we know too much about them in our present media-dominated environment. No one knew what Washington and Lincoln did every day, much less every minute of the day. Incredible as it now seems, Franklin Roosevelt served more than three terms as president without the majority of people even aware that he could not walk.

As a first step toward grasping the real meaning of leadership—and more important, as a step toward becoming an effective leader yourself—your present view of leadership may need to be reconsidered, reinvented, and even reborn. This book will give you the tools for doing that. By making full use of those tools, you can take a big step toward achieving all your personal and professional goals.

This raises a very important point that should be emphasized here at the outset. Our purpose here is something much more than theoretical or intellectual understanding of leadership. You're going to learn what leaders have done so that you can start doing it yourself, right away, in your own life and career. That's *leadership mastery*. It's putting what you learn into action.

This is an extremely ambitious undertaking, and we have some powerful tools to bring it to a successful conclusion. Very simply put, the foundations of our work toward leadership mastery are the insights, writings, and life example of Dale Carnegie. Known the world over as one of the most influential voices in the history of personal development, his lessons are more relevant today than ever before.

We'll be looking at up-to-the-minute issues in today's fast-changing workplace. We'll meet the people, study the organizations, and identify the challenges they face, and that you're facing, on the road to professional success and personal fulfillment.

THE LONGEVITY OF LEVI STRAUSS

Levi Strauss & Co. has been in business for more than 150 years. Over those many decades there have been plenty of peaks and valleys such as the great San Francisco earthquake of 1906, which destroyed the company showroom and many local businesses.

Despite the obvious hardships, the company continued to pay its employees while new buildings were built, and extended credit to its wholesale suppliers whose facilities had also been destroyed. Ethical leadership has always been a core value at Levi Strauss, whether the challenge was a major earthquake or competition from Calvin Klein. In keeping with an "aspiration statement" that the company issued in 1987, managers at Levi Strauss know that they're evaluated in many other areas besides financial performance.

As much as 40 percent of Levi Strauss's management bonuses are based on measures of leadership in ethics, human relations, and effective communication.

IBM: BUSINESS AND BELIEFS

More than twenty years before Levi Strauss created its aspiration statement, Thomas J. Watson, Jr., then the head of IBM, wrote a book called *A Business and Its Beliefs*. Watson knew that one of his most vital responsibilities as a leader was to clarify the core values of IBM. The values he led by made IBM one of America's truly dominant companies throughout the '50s, '60s, and '70s.

Interestingly enough, years before he wrote the book, Watson foresaw the problems that would almost cause IBM's downfall when the technological revolution dawned. Thirty years before anyone had ever heard of a blog or a Web site or an e-mail, Watson told an interviewer, "I'm worried that IBM could become a big inflexible organization that won't be able to change when the computer business goes through its next shift." In fact, that's exactly what happened after Watson's retirement. IBM did not fully recover until another leadership master, Louis V. Gerstner, Jr., became chairman and CEO in 1993. And we'll have much more to say about Gerstner in the chapters that follow.

JOHNSON & JOHNSON: BIG BUT SMALL

Levi Strauss and IBM are big corporations. Johnson & Johnson is as well, but the former leader of that company, chairman and CEO Ralph Larsen, has said, "We don't view ourselves as one $20 billion health care company; we see ourselves as 170 small ones." This puts into practice one of the basic principles of leadership mastery. Larsen had a strong aversion to top-down edicts and directives. "We have a strong history of decentralization," he told an interviewer. "People are very independent at Johnson & Johnson. You have to convince them of the rightness of your cause. Otherwise not much is going to happen."

Larsen might have added that once the rightness of the cause has been made clear, a lot of good things happen year in and year out. Virtually from its beginnings, Johnson & Johnson has been one of America's most admired companies, as well as one of the most profitable. With Dale Carnegie's timeless lessons providing the core of our strategy, and with tactics drawn from the example of today's leadership masters, we are ready to move ahead in our exploration of this vitally important subject.

GATES AND JOBS

The names of two men will always be linked to the technological innovations that transformed our lives in the late twentieth century. It's hard to believe that Bill Gates and Steven Jobs are now "senior citizens" of the computer age, but it's the truth. From the start their contributions were very different from one another, and they're still different today. Gates has to some extent withdrawn from the operational side of Microsoft, and is concentrating on philanthropic endeavors throughout the world. Steve Jobs, on the other hand, has been a very hands-on manager at Apple Computer. In fact, he's so involved that shareholders become extremely nervous at any signs that he might be backing off. Coverage of his recent health issues have demonstrated that.

Later in the book we'll have more to say about these two very strong leaders, who are also equally strong rivals. It remains to be seen which of the two men's legacies will be the more enduring. Perhaps surprisingly, one test of this may be which man was able to disengage more smoothly. We usually evaluate leaders in terms of how much they do, not how they transition to doing less. There's a lesson here: What leaders mean to us changes with time just as the leaders themselves change.

APPLYING THE WISDOM OF JAMES GLEICK

James Gleick, a science writer whose books have introduced readers to the wonders of chaos theory and superstrings, published a volume entitled *Faster*. Gleick discusses the seemingly unstoppable acceleration of all aspects of our lives, from the introduction of e-mail and cell phones to the raising of the speed limits on interstate highways. We have the tools to accomplish things very quickly these days and we've come to expect almost instantaneous results. As we make our way at lightning speed through our new environment, though, we must realize that our approaches, our ideas, and even our vocabularies must also be new.

The word *leader*, for example, can no longer bear any resemblance to the word *boss*. Bosses have subordinates or subjects or followers. Today's true leaders have no followers in the conventional sense of the word. Leadership masters even go a step further by transforming followers into other leaders. For true leadership masters, this process includes not just everyone in an organization, but literally everyone they meet. How does this happen?

For starters it requires personal qualities beyond traditional leadership virtues: qualities like toughness and decision-making ability, flexibility, innovation, and the ability to accommodate sudden change. These traits are now absolutely essential. The image of the leader as a lion tamer with a chair and a whip can no longer work for any extended period of time, if indeed it ever could. So the purpose of leadership mastery is not to show you how to order people around, or to manipulate them with fear of failure or promise of reward. Instead you'll focus on giving people the tools to lead themselves in the direction of what they do best.

Traditionally it's been said that some people are born leaders just as certain wolves or baboons naturally assume dominant positions in their groups. There's a view that certain human beings are simply destined by their genetic makeup to take responsibility and point the way for others. That's one way of looking at it.

But another view says that leaders aren't born, they're made. It's not in the genes. It's in the experience and in the training. This suggests that anybody can be a leader if he or she gets the necessary training and preparation. A person may be in the back of the line today, but with the right kind of attitude, knowledge, skills, and experience, that same person can be out in front of the pack tomorrow.

Which one of these theories is correct? Fortunately we don't really have to answer that question because there's a basic flaw in both possibilities. Each describes leadership as a stage of development we arrive at, whether through heredity or training. However, today the biggest challenge of leadership is not to move from a starting point to a state of expertise beyond anyone else. Rather, today's leader must find a way to keep the mind-set of the starting point no matter how far along the track he or she may have run.

Leadership mastery is about seeing people, environments, and circumstances freshly, as if for the first time. The truth is, we really are seeing everything for the first time because, as James Gleick points out, everything is constantly changing at an ever-increasing rate of speed. In fact, leadership masters are so free of preconceived ideas that they even question the validity of leadership itself (at least in the old-fashioned sense of the word). Great leaders of the past were seen as indispensable to the success of their groups. But today's great leaders realize that no one is indispensable, not even themselves.

It wasn't always that way. Many centuries ago, when Alexander the Great led his armies in conquest of much of the known world, a great battle was about to take place between the Greeks and the forces of the Persian Empire. The Persians had assembled a huge force, one that outnumbered the Greeks by as many as ten to one. On the night before the battle, however, Alexander assembled his troops and declared his absolute confidence that victory would be theirs, regardless of the numbers. He offered three basic reasons that the Greeks would win.

First he said, "Greece was a harsher environment than Persia." Second, because of the demands of simply surviving, let alone creating a great civilization, in Greece, the Greek soldiers were much tougher man-for-man than the Persians, regardless of the numbers. But the third reason for Alexander's confidence was the most important one, the one that he really emphasized to his troops, and the one that inspired them to win one of the most decisive military engagements in the history of the world. "The real difference between our army and the Persians," Alexander said, "is that they have their emperor for a leader and you have me."

In the ancient world there's no doubt that this expression of total confidence in destiny on the part of a leader was an effective strategy. In fact, it may have continued to be effective as recently as the '60s and '70s, although the benefits of this approach were clearly diminishing. Consider this: When George Steinbrenner first gained control of the New York Yankees, his dictatorial style of personal leadership quickly became evident. There was continuous news coverage of his feuds with players and managers such as Reggie Jackson, Billy Martin, and even Hall of Famer Yogi Berra (whom Steinbrenner abruptly fired as Yankee manager only sixteen games into a season).

In those days, Steinbrenner's team continued to win championships despite his overbearing leadership. Then interestingly something seemed to change in the national consciousness. People no longer responded to a rigid military model of leadership based on threat and intimidation. In the case of the New York Yankees, the stream of pennant-winning seasons came to an end until, much to his credit, Steinbrenner formed a new type of relationship with his players and his managers. He gave much more control to and empowered the men on the field. He was much more forgiving of setbacks in their play and their personal lives. As the players experienced these changes, the Yankee team of the late '90s was favorably compared with the greatest baseball dynasties of all time.

Instead of being criticized for his tyrannical despotism, George Steinbrenner was praised for his enlightened leadership. The message is clear: In today's environment, a highly personalized, individually centered, crudely aggressive leadership style is almost never effective, and certainly not over any extended period. Of course there are still people in leadership positions today who take issue with this. There are authoritarian leaders in every field who still see themselves as generals or cowboys. Some of these old-style leaders can point to very good results over the last year or the last two or three years.

In today's world, however, it is almost impossible for a purely authoritarian style of leadership to remain successful over the long term. People just won't put up with it. And society has changed so that they don't have to.

OLD-STYLE LEADERS CANNOT SURVIVE TODAY

At the height of his leadership days, John D. Rockefeller said,

The ability to deal with people is as purchasable a commodity as sugar or coffee and I will pay more for that ability than for any other under the sun.

Well, exactly what kind of leadership would Rockefeller want to pay for? We've just spoken about the fact that a high-pressure, high-stress environment is not something that people will accept from a leader today. There's another reason why old-style leaders can't survive today, and it doesn't have anything to do with the pressure they put on other people. It has everything to do with the pressure they put on themselves in a fast-changing, complex, and even chaotic world. There's nothing to be gained by claiming to know all the answers, even if you can fool other people into believing you. There's no way you can fool yourself, and living a lie can be very tiring.

Dealing with people is probably the biggest problem you face, especially if you're in the corporate world. This is also true if you're a housewife, architect, or engineer. Research done under the auspices of the Carnegie Foundation for the Advancement of Teaching uncovered an important and significant fact.

These investigations revealed that even in such technical lines as engineering, about 15 percent of one's financial success is due to one's technical knowledge and about 85 percent is due to skill in human engineering: the personality and the ability to lead people. The individual who has technical knowledge plus the ability to express ideas, assume leadership, and arouse enthusiasm among people is the person headed for higher earning power. That's one piece of the leadership puzzle. Here are some others that today's leaders need:

- *Legitimate authority.* Leaders may be elected, appointed, or simply and spontaneously recognized by the members of a group. In one way or another, all human beings are hardwired for leadership. We may want to lead or we may want to be led—but an instinct for authority exists in all of us.

  We look for a person who has a vision, who knows how to communicate it, and who can make that vision our own. Very often this takes place through the medium of forceful language, but communication through action is even more effective. Leaders know how to recognize a moment when the group is ready to receive a message, and leaders take advantage of that moment.

During the Civil War, when the Union Army was in retreat after another unsuccessful incursion into the South, the soldiers suddenly saw their new commander—General Ulysses S. Grant—turn the column around and head back into enemy territory. Grant did not announce what he was going to do. He just did it, which was much more eloquent and effective. This was literally the turning point of the war.

The identity of leader is something much larger than his identity as an individual. He or she is the embodiment of the identity of the group. He or she is the person to whom others look for advice and counsel—and when they receive it, they literally feel as if it had come from within themselves.

Again, a leader's ability to speak well is often an important part of this process. But what's really essential is the leader's inner vision. He or she must be able to forcefully communicate this vision, either by word or deed. Once this takes place, the group is won over and even doubters fall into line. Legitimate authority is conferred.

- *Authentic self-belief.* Leaders genuinely believe in themselves. This is absolutely essential for others to believe in them as well. Leaders think, feel, and know they have the power to rise above challenges and make positive results possible.

    Very often this belief in themselves is grounded in the leader's own technical expertise. A great surgeon, for example, feels confident about mentoring medical students because he or she has performed many actual surgeries over the course of a career. But this isn't always true. Some great football coaches never played football. Someone can teach a concert pianist without being able to play the instrument at a professional level. Highly effective leaders may not be very skilled or talented themselves, but they know how to recognize and inspire those who are.

Leaders are generally familiar with all the aspects of their business and understanding how things work. They are aware of what goes on from the front lines to the executive level. This wide perspective, combined with a meticulous attention to detail, allows them to recognize problems and opportunities that other miss.

- *Confidence with flexibility.* Strong leaders must be confident in the positions on key issues. They have convictions, not just opinions, especially where matters of integrity are involved. However, they are not stubborn. Leaders have the ability to really listen, which is essential for the ability to change.

  Business strategies that work well today might not tomorrow, and a leader must be quick to recognize this. Because the organization will have to adapt, the leader must learn new skills and explore new approaches even before the need arises.

  A leader must not lose sight of his purpose or the purpose of those under his charge; if he does, he risks becoming out-of-date and bringing others down with him. Leaders need foresight to bring about change and steer others toward it. They also need to be alert for unexpected turns in the road. The message is clear: Be aware of the landscape, and know how you might need to adjust.

- *Acceptance of risk.* Fear of failure causes many people to avoid taking chances. By itself, this risk aversion is not necessarily a bad thing. But if the benefits of success outweigh the chances of failing, a leader needs to take the chance. When the risk is worth taking, leaders must accept the risk.

Once the risk/benefit determination has been made, leaders must set an example for the rest of the group. If you have analyzed the risk and decided it is worth taking, you need to overcome any mental barriers that might prevent you from becoming a model for the rest of your group. To a large extent, this is a matter of preparation. The better prepared you are, the less risky a situation will be.

- *Determination.* Leaders don't give up without a fight. Successes do not always come easily, but leaders keep trying and trying again until they and their group succeed. At the same time, leaders are aware that not every battle can be won by persistence alone. Some people just don't have the ability to play in the National Basketball Association. Most of us won't be able to be professional opera singers, no matter how much we practice. Those self-limiting situations, however, are relatively few and far between. Leaders know that the vast majority of goals are achievable if the desire is strong enough, and they act accordingly.

  As a leader, you will be expected to make hard decisions when others shy away from them. Whether that means letting someone go or making dramatic changes that affect your company, you are the one who must push it through. A wishy-washy leader often fails to get things done and has a tendency to be taken advantage of. Be merciless when the business requires you to be and stick to your decisions.

ACTION STEPS

1. In the space below, write the names of the first three figures who come to mind when you think of the word *leader*.

These can be men and women in politics, the arts, or business. They can be from the present or past.

A. _____

B. _____

C. _____

2. Go back into the list you created above, and write out the effective leadership attributes that each possesses.

3. Go through the list of attributes of effective leaders that you created in #2. Put a ✓ beside those that you already possess and an X beside those that you would like to cultivate in yourself. Then create an action plan to develop these skills in yourself. You may want to add to the list as you continue reading the chapters that follow.

Communication is built on trusting relationships.

—Dale Carnegie

CHAPTER 2

Communication and Expectation

Powerful leaders can affect thousands or even millions of individuals. Whether a leader touches only one individual or many, the power that he or she has to change the world can never be underestimated. Consider Annie Sullivan, Helen Keller's wondrous teacher. The focus of her leadership was merely one child, but inadvertently, the work that she did with Helen has affected millions.

Leadership ability doesn't automatically come with the title of manager, supervisor, or team leader. It must be an ongoing learning process. Ask questions, observe carefully, and reassess the use of your resources regularly. Use your strengths, talents, and common sense.

Here are some specifics.

- *Focus on the big picture.* Understand how the work your team performs fits into the productivity, image, and overall success of the company. Plan long-term strategies for your department and communicate them to superiors and staff members. Set realistic and measurable individual and team goals, and communicate your expectations in the context of the big picture.

- *Be ambitious.* Being ambitious doesn't have to mean being cutthroat and aggressive. Use your ambition wisely. You shouldn't climb the corporate ladder by stepping on other people. Know where you want to go in your career and accept opportunities and challenges. Groom potential successors. If you're seen as irreplaceable in your particular position, you will not be promoted.

- *Know yourself.* Recognize your strengths and work on your weaknesses. Never be afraid of asking questions or taking additional training. You don't need to know everything or be the best. If you're weak on detail work, make sure you have people on your team who excel in that. Surround yourself with people who make the company look good, not "yes men" who say only what they think you want to hear.

- *Be decisive.* Plan for the unexpected and nothing will surprise you. If you've thought of the things that could go wrong with a project, you'll be able to make confident decisions on corrective action when necessary.

- *Control stress.* If you feel you have to control something, make it your stress level. As the old saying goes: "Never let them see you sweat." Have confidence in yourself and you'll inspire others to have confidence in you.

- *Accept criticism.* Demonstrate your self-confidence by accepting other people's negative comments without becoming defensive, arrogant, or submissive. Look for something useful and constructive in any criticism and thank the person. Show your professionalism and maturity.

- *Listen.* Always take an interest in hearing others' opinions. Learn what policies or problems hinder your team from doing its job effectively, efficiently, and enthusiastically. Listen carefully to better understand quality of life and work/life balance issues and then encourage employee-driven solutions.

- *Be flexible.* A strong leader doesn't always want or need to be right. Be open to dissenting opinions, other ideas, and new initiatives. If your staff members feel comfortable offering suggestions and are involved in developing and implementing some of them, they will actively look for opportunities to improve the company.

- *Be supportive.* Be patient and work through frustrations regarding people who are less dedicated and driven than you. Always treat your coworkers and staff with courtesy and respect and take an interest in them as individuals. Remember: How you interact with people impacts how you are perceived as a leader.

- *Encourage people.* A strong leader has the ability to inspire and energize. Learn to be a mentor. Concentrate on bringing out the best in people, developing their talents, and encouraging them to use their initiative and judgment.

- *Celebrate success.* Be quick to praise. A handwritten note—on decent paper, not a sticky note—congratulating and thanking an employee for a job particularly well done will earn loyalty. When things go wrong, never criticize an employee publicly. Do it quietly and constructively and, unless you're building a case for dismissal, point out something positive as well. If, in spite of their long hours and imaginative ideas, your work group's project bid was not the winning one, involve everyone in a debriefing and decide together what could be done differently next time. Then review what you've all learned together.

- *Back your staff.* Being a leader doesn't automatically mean people will follow you. You need to show that you're behind them. Understand your team's needs. Whether it's increased training, upgraded tools, new technology, or a shift in duties, be willing to fight for them. You won't always be successful, but it's important that you act as their advocate.

- *Help out.* Pitch in whenever you can, even if it's only for a few minutes. Show them that you understand their challenges, even if you're not experienced at doing their jobs. You'll be better able to clarify expectations and do meaningful performance reviews if you have up-to-date and hands-on knowledge of their duties and responsibilities.

- *Accept responsibility.* The buck stops with you. If a shipment was late or information on a project was incorrect, be ready to take responsibility for your staff's errors, apologize, and take corrective action. Whose fault it was does not matter at this point; deal with the employee responsible for it afterward.

- *Solve problems.* As a leader, you'll need to make difficult, sometimes unpopular decisions. You'll need to manage conflict and help people accept change. Communication is the key. If you are committed to your career, your duties, and your work group, you'll find innovative ways to resolve problems.

- *Lead by example.* Always show your ability to work well with others, no matter how much you might differ in opinions and approaches. Be fair and don't play favorites. Keep negative comments and frustrations to yourself. Maintain a positive attitude, no matter what.

- *Do the right thing.* When you're faced with a decision that goes against your own values, speak up. If you're asked to do something illegal or unethical, refuse. Stand up for yourself and for the rights of your employees or work group.

- *Be honest.* If you cannot live up to a promise, don't make that promise in the first place. When you make a mistake, admit it and apologize. With so much emphasis these days on spin and damage control, you'll impress your superiors, clients, and staff if you're honest.

- *Avoid gossip.* Don't spread malicious rumors or repeat seemingly inconsequential stories about other people. It takes a strong person to say "I don't like talking about someone who's not here," but it shows integrity. Demonstrate and inspire respect and you'll also avoid creating opportunities for anyone to gossip about you.

- *Do your best.* It sounds so simple, doesn't it? Maintain confidentiality, respect others, and be consistent. Always offer your best talents and skills for any project, and you'll earn admiration and respect for your unfailing commitment and integrity.

- *Criticize constructively.* Effective leadership, especially when dealing with another's sense of dignity and pride, takes subtlety, empathy, and tact. Whether practiced by a famous world leader or a prolific and inspiring teacher, the principles and practices that create an outstanding leader remain the same. Begin with praise and honest appreciation. Call attention to people's mistakes, but find a way to do so indirectly. Talk about your own mistakes before criticizing the other person. Ask questions instead of giving direct orders. Let the other person save face. Praise the slightest improvement and praise every improvement. Be hearty in your approval and lavish in your praise. Give the other person a fine reputation to live up to. Use encouragement. Make the fault seem easy to correct. Make the other person happy about doing the things you suggest.

When communicated correctly, positively directing others toward personal or professional improvement is invaluable.

THE POWER OF GOOD COMMUNICATION

Leadership mastery is a combination of many skills. There is one thing that a leader must be able to do skillfully and articulately. Very simply stated, leaders must be able to communicate. At the outset of this book, it's vital for us to look closely at what's involved in effective communication, about what it is and what it is not.

Communication has always taken many forms. Just in the past few years important new media for communication have emerged. So when we refer to communication we're not limited to speech. We're talking about e-mail and snail mail. We're talking about cell phones and videoconferencing. But even as more avenues for communication emerge, certain basic truths have proven themselves again and again. In fact, many of these principles were identified and explained by Dale Carnegie himself. And he was especially insightful in the area of leadership communication.

Mr. Carnegie found, for example, that effective leaders open many challenging conversations with sincere praise and honest appreciation. Please take special note of the words *sincere praise* and *honest appreciation*. A manager who calls someone into his office, woodenly recites a few words of praise, and then erupts in anger or recrimination will not accomplish very much. As a leader about to initiate a difficult conversation in the business setting, give some thought to what you can honestly say to the other party that conveys respect and appreciation. It doesn't even have to be directly related to the topic at hand. If a manager is going to talk with an employee about meeting deadlines or quarterly goals, the conversation can begin by praising an insightful comment the employee made in a meeting recently. The content of the positive message is relatively unimportant compared to its sincerity and honesty.

Dale Carnegie also realized that sometimes a leader needs to offer constructive criticism. When this becomes necessary it's best to call attention to someone's mistakes indirectly. Sometimes the best way to do this is by referring to a mistake of your own. If you bluntly state that someone has done something wrong and they better not do it again, they're going to react much more strongly to your threatening tone than to the content of what you've said.

If, however, you can identify with the person you're talking to, and show that you too have occasionally fallen short in a similar situation, you'll reduce the level of resistance to the important message you are there to convey. By allowing people to save face and retain self-respect, a leader can head off the negative feelings that lead to dissension and poor performance.

HOW AND WHEN TO GIVE PRAISE

As careful as a leader should be when administering criticism, you can freely lavish praise almost anywhere and at any time. In fact, even slight improvements in attitude or performance should receive immediate positive attention. This is one of Dale Carnegie's most valuable insights. If we're trying to encourage complex forms of performance from people (and many jobs today are indeed complex and demanding), we shouldn't wait until the task is done perfectly before offering praise and encouragement. When even small signs of improvement or heightened effort appear, that's reason enough for an effective leader to take notice.

Sometimes, in fact, offering praise can be of enormous benefit even before tangible signs of improvement appear. As Dale Carnegie described it, "Providing someone with a reputation to live up to can be the best way of inspiring peak performance." Often when a person has achieved a leadership position, there's a temptation to devalue the capabilities of everyone else. After all, if you're the leader, it must be because you have superior and perhaps unique capabilities, right? This line of thinking can cause you to underestimate the achievements of subordinates.

A GOOD LEADER DELEGATES

Many leaders simply wait too long before delegating power. This not only reduces the efficiency of organizations but also withholds opportunities for growth among people who are ready to make a greater contribution. One of the paradoxes of organizations is their relationship to stability and change. On one hand, all complex systems naturally seek to achieve balance. If the temperature is in the nineties, people tend to perspire. This is the body's way of cooling the surface of the skin in an attempt to balance the effects of the high temperature of the air.

In a similar way, organizations that find themselves under stress may become conservative and defensive in their responses, as if the best way to deal with external change is to minimize change internally. Impulses in this direction can cause leaders to consolidate too much power for themselves or to hold on to power too long. To move beyond this limiting mind set, it's important to realize that an affinity for balance is natural only until balance has been achieved. After that, nature begins to move in the other direction, toward innovation and change. So many organizations and so many people manage to achieve leadership positions as a result of their creativity and originality. Often, though, they then seem to forsake the very talents that got them to the top in the first place.

They begin thinking and acting defensively. Once that happens, it is no longer a question of whether they'll lose their leadership positions. It is only a question of when.

In summing up the leadership master's approach to communication, we need to emphasize the importance of putting everything, even criticism, within a proactive, positive framework: a framework that recognizes the universal human need for recognition and appreciation. The leader must understand the true importance of the idea that success is a journey rather than a destination. Success requires continuous innovation and creative thinking. This is especially true when you've already achieved some success, and you are tempted to become conservative and defensive.

EMBRACING NEW IDEAS

Akio Morita built Sony into one of the world's most profitable and innovative companies. In response to a leader's tendency toward conservatism, Morita said, "If you go through life convinced that your way is always best, all the new ideas in the world will pass you by." Not many new ideas passed by Sony under Morita's leadership. His company introduced Japan's first commercial transistor radio, the 3.5-inch floppy disk, and the Walkman. In 1978, Morita came up with the idea of the Walkman when he wanted to listen to opera on long airplane trips. This began the whole portable entertainment revolution, replaced today by the MP3 player and the iPod. A striking instance of creative leadership, the Walkman was developed with a minimum of market research and testing. "I don't believe any amount of research could have predicted its success," said Morita in an interview. "The public doesn't always know what it's possible to do."

Socrates said repeatedly to his followers in Athens, "One thing only I know and that is that I know nothing." We can't hope to be any smarter than Socrates, so we would be wise to quit telling people they're wrong. In the end it pays off. If a person makes a statement that you think is wrong, isn't it better to begin by saying, "Well, now look, I thought otherwise but I may be wrong. I frequently am, and if I am wrong I want to be put right. Let's examine the facts." There's magic, positive magic, in such phrases as "I may be wrong, I frequently am, let's examine the facts."

People often find themselves in careers far removed from what they really hope for and expect. Many feel alienated from their work but they continue, because they don't really see an alternative. That is, until someone offers them a chance to use their talents as they'd really wanted to in the first place. Sometimes it's a leadership master who presents that opportunity, and sometimes they have to discover it for themselves.

Dale Carnegie belongs in the second category. He had trained to become a teacher at a state college in Missouri, yet as a young man he somehow found himself selling trucks in New York City. If that seems like an unlikely turn of events, it's no more unlikely than aspiring novelists who turn into corporate lawyers, or gourmet cooks who become accountants. One day it dawned on Mr. Carnegie that he was living a life totally unrelated to the one he had envisioned for himself. This was a very unsettling realization, but unlike many people, Dale Carnegie decided to do something about it.

The first step he took was quitting his job as a truck salesman. That took some fortitude, but it was something he had wanted to do for a long time. The next step was a bit more complicated. Mr. Carnegie knew he did not want to sell trucks, and that his training had been in education. He saw that what he really wanted to do was write. As he considered his training and his aspirations, a plan began to form in his mind. Perhaps he could find work as an instructor in adult education classes held at night. He could then have his days free to fashion novels and short stories. It was a good idea but it was not as simple as it seemed.

Mr. Carnegie first applied to the most prestigious institutions of higher learning in the Manhattan area, including Columbia and New York University. Both schools, as he later described it, "somehow decided they could get along without me." Finally a job teaching adult classes on salesmanship and public speaking skills opened up at the night school of the YMCA.

MOTIVATION

We all crave appreciation and recognition and we will do almost anything to get it. However, nobody wants insincerity. Nobody wants flattery. These principles will work only when they come from the heart. We are not advocating a bag of tricks, but are talking about a new way of life. We are talking about changing people. If you can inspire the people with whom you come in contact to a realization of the hidden treasures they possess, you can do far more than changing them. You can literally transform them. Does this sound like an exaggeration? Then listen to these sage words from William James, one of the most distinguished psychologists and philosophers America has ever produced. "Compared with what we ought to be, we are only half awake. We're making use of only a small part of our physical and mental resources. Stating the thing broadly, the human individual thus lives far within his limits. He possesses powers of various sorts which he habitually fails to use." Yes, you who are reading these lines possess powers of various sorts which you habitually fail to use; and one of these powers you are probably not using to the fullest extent is your magic ability to praise people and inspire them with a realization of their latent possibilities. Abilities wither under criticism. They blossom under encouragement.

ACTION STEPS

1. Listed below are the nine principles to effective leadership. Go through these principles and put a ✓ by those that you believe you have mastered, and put an X by those that you would like to further develop. Then map out an action plan to integrate them into your leadership communications.

   - Principle One: Begin with praise and honest appreciation.

   - Principle Two: Call attention to people's mistakes indirectly.

   - Principle Three: Talk about your own mistakes before criticizing the other person.

   - Principle Four: Ask questions instead of giving direct orders.

   - Principle Five: Let the other person save face.

   - Principle Six: Praise the slightest improvement and praise every improvement. Be hearty in your approbation and lavish in your praise.

   - Principle Seven: Give the other person a fine reputation to live up to.

   - Principle Eight: Use encouragement. Make the fault seem easy to correct.

   - Principle Nine: Make the other person happy about doing the thing you suggest.

2. Dale Carnegie's early beginnings are intriguing. He noted that being a truck salesman neither motivated him nor fulfilled his desires. He decided to focus on his passion, and take a course of action toward that dream. How fulfilled do you currently feel in the work that you do?

3. Are you are using your magical abilities to praise people and inspire them with a realization of their latent possibilities? Write down three "magical" things that you can do to further inspire those around you on an ongoing basis.

True enthusiasm is made up of two parts: eagerness and assurance.

—Dale Carnegie

CHAPTER 3

Motivation That Empowers

We spoke in the previous chapters about communication as the first all-important element of leadership mastery. In this chapter we'll look more closely at the goals that good communication means to accomplish. At the simplest level, of course, there's the straightforward exchange of information. All leaders must provide the necessary, practical tools for accomplishing this objective. They must say what needs to be done, when, and how. It is surprising how difficult even this seems to be for many people. Beneath the surface or between the lines of truly masterful leadership communication, however, there is a deeper purpose. In a word, it is motivation.

A MOTIVATOR VERSUS AN ORATOR

Several years ago an executive retreat was held for senior managers in a Fortune 500 company. On the first day of the retreat there were two brief talks, the first by the chief executive officer, and the second by the chief operating officer of the company. In the intermission after the CEO spoke, there was general admiration in the audience for what he had said and how he said it. There was no doubt that his had been an eloquent and informative talk. Then it came time for the chief operating officer to speak. When he was finished, there was another intermission. This time, no one referred to the eloquence or the volume of information in the talk. Instead everyone in the audience seemed to have the same reaction. They were saying, "We've got work to do. Let's get going."

The difference between those two talks was the difference between oratory and rhetoric (or good public speaking) and genuine motivation. The response to good public speaking is, "What a beautiful speech," whereas the response to an effective motivational speech is, "Let's get to work." The second response is, of course, what leadership masters need to achieve, whether it's in their speeches or in everything else they undertake. Louis B. Mayer, head of MGM Pictures during the golden age of Hollywood, used to appear unannounced on the sets of movies in production. On one occasion he strolled onto a film set and found the director, the cameraman, and the actors all standing around looking worried.

"What's the matter?" Mayer asked. The director said, "Sir, we're having trouble shooting this scene. We're not sure what to do." Mayer turned bright red and thundered, "Well, do anything. If you do something right, we'll use it, and if you do something wrong, we'll fix it. But do something and do it now." What he meant was, get motivated. And simply getting into action is the first step. But leadership masters know there's more to it than that. Motion may be nothing more than spinning your wheels unless it's accompanied by some other very important elements.

ENGAGING THE BODY, HEART, AND MIND

Action may be wasted energy, or even self-destructive in the absence of two other fundamental components. Let's be very clear about this. Real motivation requires action, plus emotion, plus intelligence. To put it another way, motivation must engage the body, the heart, and the mind. Leadership masters can touch all three of these elements. They can engage us at every level of our lives. In terms of pure technique, motivation can express itself in three basic forms: negative motivation; positive motivation to motivate others; and the unique, highly individualized techniques you need to motive yourself. It's important for a leadership master to understand all these categories. So let's look at them one by one.

The Pitfalls of Negative Motivation

Although all forms of motivation have their place, negative motivation is the most limited form, which is a bit surprising since it's the approach that many leaders tend to rely on. They rely on it heavily and sometimes even exclusively. This is a big mistake. True, criticism or the threat of punishment can be somewhat effective. The possibility of firing or demoting someone can get his or her attention, but much research has shown that negative motivators have very serious limitations, especially over the long term.

In the past, loudness was often equated with toughness. Stubbornness was equated with superior knowledge. Willingness to argue was equated with honesty. We should all be grateful that those days are coming to an end. As a leader you should make it your business to see that they don't come back. A Midwestern insurance man we'll call Fred is a prime illustration of the problems with old-fashioned, negative motivation. Fred's official title is regional sales manager, but behind his back he's known as the boss who cried wolf. Four times a year, like clockwork, Fred looks at the quarterly sales figures and immediately threatens to fire everyone.

He turns bright red, hits the ceiling, and slams his fist onto his desk. Unfortunately for him, the firm's employees now treat Fred's tirades as pure theater. In fact, they jokingly assign his explosions numerical ratings on their Richter scale. Over the years, more than one representative has gotten tired of the drama and simply jumped ship. This has cost Fred's company some good people. If Fred's negative style was ever effective, that time has long passed. That's the trouble with negative motivational techniques in general.

If you follow through with them, you eventually destroy morale and create enmity within the organization. On the other hand, if you don't follow through, people quickly learn to tune out. Dale Carnegie addressed this issue very clearly. He once said there was only one way under heaven to get anyone to do anything and that is by making the other person want to do it. Mr. Carnegie, of course, was referring to the supreme importance of positive motivation. He went on to say that you could make someone want to give you his watch by sticking a gun in his ribs. You can make your employees give you cooperation at least for a little while by threatening to fire them. But these crude methods have sharply undesirable repercussions.

LEADERSHIP DEVELOPMENT TIPS

Leadership is about behavior first and skills second. People respond to leaders who inspire trust and respect, rather than to the skills they possess. In this sense, leadership is different from management, which relies more on planning, organization, and communication skills. Leadership includes management skills too, but leadership's foundation contains qualities such as integrity, honesty, humility, courage, commitment, sincerity, passion, confidence, wisdom, determination, compassion, sensitivity, and personal charisma.

Leadership comes in many different styles. A leader's personal style may be right for certain situations and wrong for others. Others are able to adapt and use different leadership styles for a variety of challenges.

Someone new to a leadership role may feel pressure to lead in a particularly dominant way. Dominant leadership is rarely appropriate, however, especially in well-established organizations. Misreading this situation can cause problems for a new leader. Resistance from the constituents becomes a problem, and a cycle of discontent and reduced performance may get started.

So much of leadership is paradoxical. It's often more about serving than leading. Teams respond best to gratitude, encouragement, recognition, and inclusiveness. Tough, dominant leadership gives people a lot to push against and resist. It also blocks any sense of ownership and empowerment among those being led. Yes, leaders need to make tough decisions, but in the day-to-day world a leader should most concentrate on enabling the team to thrive and grow. This is actually a serving role, not the dominant style usually associated with authority.

Today ethical leadership is more important than ever, and there's a very practical reason for this. The world is more transparent and connected than it has ever been. The actions and philosophies of organizations are scrutinized as never before. At the same time, there is a much greater awareness of and interest in corporate responsibility—in finance, in diversity, and in environmental issues. A modern leader needs to understand and lead in all these areas.

LEADERSHIP PHILOSOPHY

A leader's philosophy is simply the fundamental purposes and principles with which he or she identifies. It's the foundation for strategy, management, operational activities, and pretty much everything else that happens in an organization. Regardless of the size of an organization, everything that takes place under a leader's direction needs to be congruent with a clearly defined philosophy.

Executives, managers, staff, customers—they all need solid

philosophical principles on which to base their expectations, decisions, and actions. In a complex organization, leadership will be very challenging at the best of times due to size, diversity, or other issues. A conflicted philosophy dramatically increases these difficulties for everyone, and certainly for the leader, because the frame of reference becomes confusing.

For leadership to work well, team members must connect their expectations, aims, and activities to the basic purpose or philosophy of the organization. This philosophy can provide reference points and grounding for employees' decisions and actions—an increasingly significant factor in modern "empowered" organizations. Seeing a clear philosophy and purpose is also essential for staff, customers, and outsiders in assessing crucial organizational characteristics such as integrity, ethics, fairness, quality, and performance. A clear philosophy is vital to the psychological contract—almost always unstated—under which employees, managers, and customers initiate their decisions and actions.

Too many organizations, large and small, have conflicting and confusing fundamental aims. The lesson here is that philosophy and purpose are the foundation of leadership. If the foundation is not solid, then everything built onto it is prone to wobble, and may fall over completely.

As a leader, your responsibility extends beyond the act of leading. True leadership also includes the responsibility to protect or refine fundamental purpose and philosophy. Get the philosophy right, in harmony with the actions, and the foundation is strong.

Different leaders have different ideas about leadership. But to anyone who studies the experience of contemporary business and organizational leaders, certain points emerge. There are key principles of leadership:

- When leaders say that the people are not following, it's the leaders who are lost, not the people.

- Leaders get lost because of isolation, arrogance, or bad judgment. But above all they get lost because they become preoccupied with imposing their authority instead of truly leading.

- Leadership is helping people achieve a shared vision, not telling people what to do.

- Loyalty to leadership relies on the leader's connection and understanding of people's needs, wishes, and possibilities. Solutions to leadership challenges do not lie in the leader's needs and wishes. Leadership solutions lie in the needs and wishes of the followers.

- Loyalty can't be built by simply asking or forcing people to be loyal.

- Before expecting anyone to follow, a leader first needs to demonstrate a vision and values worthy of a following.

- Any specific type of leadership inevitably attracts the same type of followers. In other words, for people to embrace and follow modern compassionate, honest, ethical, peaceful, and fair principles, they must see these qualities demonstrated by their leadership.

- People are a lot more perceptive than most leaders think. People have a much keener sense of truth than most leaders think. People quickly lose faith in a leader who ignores these two facts.

- Often people have answers that elude their leaders. Leaders, therefore, should solicit ideas, opinions, and suggestions to gain buy-in and cultivate loyalty.

- A leader who makes mistakes should come clean and admit the errors. People will generally forgive mistakes but do not appreciate leaders who are unwilling to take responsibility for their actions.

- A leader should be brave enough to negotiate when lesser people want to fight. Anyone can resort to threats and aggression, but being aggressive is not leading.

THE NEED TO FEEL SIGNIFICANT

So what do people really want? Not really so many things according to Dale Carnegie. He enumerated several: health and the preservation of life, food and shelter, a certain amount of money and the things money will buy, the well-being of their children, and a fundamental sense of their own significance. All these things are relatively easy to gratify, Dale Carnegie continued, except for the last one. This longing is almost as deep and insistent as the desire for food and water. John Dewey called it "the desire to be important." Freud went further and called it "the desire to be great." Positive motivation means giving people a real sense of purpose, a feeling that they're working toward a valuable, attainable, and mutually important goal. There's nothing new about the concept. Leadership masters have always understood it.

During the first term of his presidency, Dwight Eisenhower was asked about his secret for dealing with a reluctant and unruly Congress. Did the former general mention military discipline or the might-makes-right power of the presidency? On the contrary, Eisenhower talked about positive motivation. "You do not lead people by hitting them on the head," he declared. "That's assault, not leadership. I would rather positively persuade a man to go along because once he's made that choice, he will stick. If I scare him, he will stay just as long as he's scared and then he'll be gone."

A Theory of Motivational Needs

Harvard professor David McClelland (1917–98) pioneered work-place motivational thinking. In his 1961 book, *The Achieving Society*, McClelland described three types of motivational need, which he identified as achievement motivation, authority-power motivation, and affiliation.

These needs are found to varying degrees in all workers and managers. The mix of motivational needs defines an individual's style and behavior, both in terms of their own motivation and in the management and motivation of others.

- *The need for achievement.* The achievement-oriented person is motivated by results and therefore seeks achievement, attainment of realistic but challenging goals, and advancement in the job. There is a strong need for feedback on achievement and progress and a need for a sense of accomplishment.

- *The need for authority and power.* This is a need to be influential, effective, and impactful. There is an intention to lead and for the person's ideas to prevail. There is also motivation and need toward increasing personal status and prestige.

- *The need for affiliation.* The affiliation-motivated person needs friendly relationships and is motivated toward interaction with other people. The affiliation driver produces motivation and a need to be liked and held in popular regard. These people are team players.

McClelland said that most people exhibit a combination of these characteristics. Some people exhibit a strong tendency for a particular motivational need, and this motivational or needs mix consequently affects their behavior and working/managing style. McClelland suggested that a strong affiliation motivation undermines a manager's objectivity, because the need to be liked affects a manager's decision-making capability.

A strong authority motivation will produce a determined work ethic and commitment to the organization. While these individuals are attracted to the leadership role, they may not possess the required flexibility and people-centered skills.

In the end, McClelland argues that people with strong achievement motivation make the best leaders, although they may demand too much of their staffs in the belief that they are all similarly and *highly* achievement focused and results driven, which of course most people are not.

In light of this, McClelland's particular fascination was for achievement motivation. A well-known laboratory experiment illustrates one aspect of his theory about the effect of achievement on people's motivation. McClelland suggested through this experiment that while most people do not possess a strong achievement-based motivation, those who do display a consistent behavior in setting goals.

Volunteers were asked to throw rings over pegs, rather like the fairground game. No distance was stipulated, and most people seemed to throw from arbitrary, random distances, sometimes close, sometimes farther away. However, a small group of volunteers, whom McClelland suggested were strongly achievement motivated, took some care to measure and test distances to produce an ideal challenge: not too easy and not impossible. A similar concept exists in biology, known as the overload principle. This is usually applied to fitness and exercising; i.e., to develop fitness and/or strength, the exercise must be sufficiently demanding to increase existing levels, but not so demanding as to cause damage or strain. McClelland identified the same need for a balanced challenge in the approach of achievement-motivated people.

McClelland contrasted achievement-motivated people with

gamblers and daredevils, and dispelled a common preconception that achievement-motivated people are big risk takers. On the contrary, achievement-motivated individuals set goals that they can influence with their effort and ability, and as such the goal is considered achievable. This determined, results-driven mind-set is almost always present in the character makeup of successful business people and entrepreneurs.

McClelland suggested other characteristics and attitudes of achievement-motivated people:

- Achievement itself is more important than material or financial reward.

- Achieving the aim or task gives greater personal satisfaction than receiving praise or recognition.

- Financial reward is regarded as a measurement of success, not an end in itself.

- Security is not a prime motivator, nor is status.

- Feedback is essential, because it enables measurement of success, not for reasons of praise or recognition (the implication here is that feedback must be reliable, quantifiable, and factual).

- Achievement-motivated people constantly seek improvements and ways of doing things better.

- Achievement-motivated people prefer jobs and responsibilities that naturally satisfy their needs, i.e., offer flexibility and the opportunity to set and achieve goals, e.g., sales and business management and entrepreneurial roles.

McClelland firmly believed that achievement-motivated people are generally the ones who make things happen and get results, and that this extends to getting results through the organization of other people and resources, although, as stated earlier, they often demand too much of their staffs because they prioritize achieving the goal above the many varied interests and needs of their people.

THREE CONCEPTS OF HUMAN BEHAVIOR

Once a leader has grasped the basic importance of positive motivation, it's relatively easy to create specific applications of the principle. But three important concepts of human behavior should be included in them all. First, everyone must be included and informed in all phases of an endeavor, at every step of the way. Teamwork is the key, not hierarchy or chain of command. Second, people must be treated as individuals. Their ideas and suggestions must be acknowledged and treated with respect. Third, superior performances must be expected, encouraged, recognized, and rewarded. And the rewards must come quickly, not just at the end of the year or at the retirement party.

Very often a personal note or a phone call from the leader means as much to a high-performing team member as a cash bonus, although the note and the cash together are sure to get quick attention. In any case, the purpose is to create a sense of inclusion and positive reinforcement. For many years, in large traditionally organized companies, there was a basic sense of disconnection. People felt like mere numbers, one of thousands, human cogs in a gigantic impersonal machine. It's hardly surprising that in these organizations employees were ready to call in sick on the slightest excuse, or spend more time on breaks during the day than at their desks. If any company's employees feel that way today, one conclusion is obvious: That company is poorly led. The organization's goals have not become the people's goals and no business can achieve success in a situation like that.

TEAMWORK IS CRITICAL

Leadership masters today involve team members in all aspects of the business. It's no longer simply a matter of issuing orders from above. Effective leaders know that team members are more than capable of making important decisions on their own and that empowering them to make these decisions is a vital form of positive motivation.

As one executive in a midsize publishing firm explained, "If I tell people how they can improve, they may take it to heart and they may not. If I don't put it the right way, there's even a chance they'll be insulted. But if I first ask how I myself can improve, they're complimented. If I put their suggestions into action, they're really proud, and if I ask them again how I can do even better, now I really have their attention. That's the time to finally make my own suggestions about what they can do also. It's only after I've made everyone feel like a leader that I can most effectively be a leader myself." So walk around, say hello, and get to know every member of your team. Above all acknowledge a job well done. Don't be the tight-lipped, disapproving parent or teacher that many people unfortunately grew up with. That kind of person is painful for a child and it's still painful for an adult.

People don't just want to be told when they're not doing well; they need to be told when they are. They need praise. They need celebration. There are literally dozens of techniques for celebrating hard work and success. An executive at a New Orleans cable company makes a conscious effort to use as many of these techniques as possible. As he describes it, "We have skits during our monthly meetings to reinforce our message and keep our goals highly visible. We also have celebrations. We've even had fireworks. We have speakers and awards to exemplify the excellence we strive for. We give away money at employee meetings—anything to get people involved and excited."

Ten Questions Leaders Should Ask Their Teams

1. What is the primary aim of our company?

Your team members will be more highly motivated if they understand the primary aim of your business. Ask questions to establish how clear they are about your company's principles, priorities, and mission. These concepts are of a higher order than simple goals. As the business author Marshall Goldsmith has pointed out, when short-term goals become an obsession, they can do more harm than good. A firm's mission is its basic philosophy and reason for being; it's not just the financial targets for the next quarter.

2. What obstacles stop team members performing to best effect?

Include questions about what obstacles to motivation do team members tolerate in their work. The company can eliminate practices that zap motivation.

3. What really motivates your staff?

It is often assumed that all people are motivated by the same things. Actually we are motivated by a whole range of factors. Include questions to elicit what really motivates team members, including financial rewards, status, recognition, competition, job security—and even fear.

4. Do team members feel empowered?

Do your team members feel they have job descriptions that empower them to find their own solutions? Or are they given a list of tasks to perform and simply told what to do?

5. *Are there any recent changes in the company that might have affected motivation?*

Has your company had layoffs, imposed a hiring freeze, or lost a number of key people? This will have an effect on motivation. Collect information from team members about their fears, thoughts, and concerns relating to these events. Even if they are unfounded, treat them with respect and honesty.

6. *What are the patterns of motivation in your company?*

Who is most motivated and why? What lessons can you learn from instances of high and low motivation in your company?

7. *Are employee goals and company goals aligned?*

First, the company needs to establish how it wants individuals to most productively spend their time. Second, this needs to be compared with how individuals actually do spend their time. You may find that team members are highly motivated—but in the wrong direction.

8. *How do team members feel about the company?*

Do they feel safe, loyal, valued, and taken care of? Or do they feel taken advantage of, dispensable, and invisible? Ask them what would improve their loyalty and commitment.

9. *How involved are team members in company development?*

Do they feel listened to and heard? Are they consulted? And, if they are consulted, are their opinions taken seriously? Are there regular opportunities for them to give feedback?

10. Is the company's internal image consistent with its external one?

Your company may present itself to the world as the "caring airline," the "forward-thinking technology company," or the "family hotel chain." But if you do not mirror this image within your firm by the way you treat team members, you may notice motivation problems. Find out what the disparity is between the team members' image of the company from the outside and from the inside.

RESPECT AND APPRECIATION GO A LONG WAY

As a leader, one of your foremost responsibilities is letting your team members know that you respect them, that you appreciate them, and that you want to help them achieve their full potential. Positive motivation is simply the best way to get these messages across. The action steps below include an exercise for listing positive motivational techniques you can implement in your leadership role. Be sure to fill it out entirely. Once you've done so, start putting your ideas into action immediately.

ACTION STEPS

1. Suppose you were speaking before a group of people about to undertake a serious physical challenge. It might be running a marathon or ten-kilometer race, climbing a mountain, or even building a house. How would you express yourself to motivate them for this activity? Write out the specific kind of challenges your audience might face. Then write a brief message designed to maximize their motivation for the task at hand.

2. Reflect on your past and recall a circumstance in which your own desire to be great was fulfilled in response to positive motivation. What was the exact form of the

motivation? How did it make you feel at the time? Do you still feel that way? Try to describe your feelings as vividly as possible.

3. Based on the teachings of this book thus far, list all of the positive motivational techniques you can begin to implement in your leadership role. Make note of those that you currently practice, and those that you do not. Then create an action plan to incorporate *all* of the tools into your routine regimen.

Most big challenges are best faced with a series of interim goals.

—Dale Carnegie

CHAPTER 4

Mentoring That Makes a Difference

So far we've spoken about motivating others, about the limits of negative motivation, and about the many benefits of more positive approaches. Our focus has been exclusively on how a leader can use these principles to motivate others. It should be clear, however, that leadership mastery also includes the ability to motivate yourself.

WELL-DEFINED GOALS

Dale Carnegie had a great deal to say about the process of self-motivation, and he very clearly identified the single most important tool for bringing this about. That tool is the creation of clear, realistic, and worthy goals. It is not exaggeration to say that goal-setting is the magic formula for optimum self-motivation. With well-defined goals, your full potential is brought into play and almost any reality-based objective can and will be achieved. In the absence of such goals, however, very little can be accomplished and most likely nothing at all.

Goals give us something to shoot for. They focus our thoughts and efforts. They also allow us to track our progress and to measure our success. So as a leader you simply must make goal-setting a top priority. You should set goals that are challenging but also achievable, and that are clear and measurable. These goals should take the form of short-term plans as well as long-term objectives. When leadership masters reach one goal, they take a moment to enjoy what they've achieved, but they've mastered the art of quickly moving on to the next objective, emboldened, strengthened, and energized by what has already been accomplished.

Eugene Lang: An Example of Powerful Goal-Setting

A dramatic example of the power of goal-setting comes from a New York City philanthropist named Eugene Lang. Like many people, Mr. Lang was not satisfied with the state of public education in his community. Unlike many people, Mr. Lang also made it an important personal goal to do something about this problem. His plan for attaining this goal included the creation of goals for the students he intended to benefit. Eugene Lang announced his plan at a graduation speech to a sixth-grade class in New York City. Statistically the children in this group had little chance of even graduating from high school, let alone going to college.

At the end of his speech, however, Mr. Lang made a stunning announcement: "For every student in this sixth-grade class who graduates from high school, I will ensure that money is available for that student to go to college: no ifs, ands, or buts." This was goal-setting and leadership at its best. Eugene Lang had a goal and out of it came other goals for an entire group of young people. The goals were clear and powerful, but were they attainable in the failure-ridden public school system? Only time would tell. As it turned out, of the 54 students who remained in contact, more than 90 percent have high school diplomas or GED certificates, and 60 percent went to college. Of course this amazing success rate wasn't brought about by the financial incentive alone.

Eugene Lang made sure that the students got counseling and support all along the way. Because of the one challenging goal Mr. Lang had set for himself, together with the goals it created for the students, dozens of lives were transformed. Impossible dreams were turned into tangible reality. Indeed, as best-selling author Napoleon Hill put it, "A goal is a dream with a deadline." People who set challenging but achievable goals have a solid grip on the future. They accomplish extraordinary things. They become leadership masters.

In the action steps at the end of this chapter you'll find exercises to help you identify your short, intermediate, and long-term goals and help you measure your progress on the way. Be sure to make use of them as soon as you can.

WHAT IT TAKES TO FIND A MENTOR

We have stressed the importance of motivating others, and we've seen how realistic goal-setting is essential for leaders to motivate themselves. For the balance of this chapter we'll look at another motivational strategy that richly deserves our attention. This is the process of mentoring: both finding a mentor and becoming one yourself.

An ancient saying tells us, "When the pupil is ready, the teacher will appear." That may very well be true, but there's another proverb that may be even older, the one that says, "Heaven helps those who themselves." Finding a mentor and being a mentor may to some extent happen naturally over the course of a leader's career, but the process can be greatly expedited by awareness, focus, and a bit of legwork.

It may take a bit of your time at first, but it's time well spent and it can also be a lot of fun. Right now let's look at what it really takes to find a mentor, or to put it another way, let's make it very clear what that process should not involve. Finding a mentor does not mean identifying someone who's very successful and simply trying to copy them. As the CEO of a major software company put it, "Every human being is like a snowflake or a fingerprint or a strand of DNA: We're all unique. We'll never find anyone exactly like us." Finding a mentor doesn't mean just wanting to impersonate somebody. Finding a mentor starts with looking beneath the surface to the essential truth of who people really are.

When the fit is right at that basic level, the real mentoring experience can begin. Bill Gates is one of the world's wealthiest individuals. But let's see what just copying the life of Bill Gates might involve. Bill Gates dropped out of college. So if you were a young person in school and you were getting a little tired of staying up late writing research papers, you might consider heading out to Silicon Valley to make your fortune. After all, that's what Bill Gates did, and you've chosen him as your mentor and model.

But it's not really that simple. Bill Gates was enrolled at Harvard University as a mathematics major. He was certainly talented in math, but it didn't take him long to realize something very important: Other students at Harvard were significantly more talented than he was. The basic reason Gates left Harvard was not because he was in a hurry to make his fortune. It was because he had a very aggressive, competitive personality. He realized he couldn't be the best in this arena, and he was getting tired of playing against the future Michael Jordans of the math world.

So he took his ball and went home. That's what Bill Gates did, at about the same time as probably dozens of people you've never heard of, individuals who will certainly never become the richest people in the world. They were probably doing the same thing: quitting. If you decide to quit in the middle of something because, after all, that's what Bill Gates did, you should also be aware that Bill Jones did that and he's flipping burgers. Bill Smith also did that, and he's bagging groceries.

So you've got to look very carefully at your choice of a mentor. Once the choice has been made, you've got to ask yourself, "Is this who I really am? Is this who I really want to be?"

Researching a Good Mentor Is Essential

In selecting a possible mentor, don't limit yourself to people you read about in the newspaper. Do some research. Zero in on people in your industry who share your concerns and have faced the same issues you're facing right now. The good news is, the technological revolution has made all this easier than ever before.

The World Wide Web is the greatest research instrument ever invented, and e-mail is the ideal way to contact the potential mentors you select. Don't be shy about this. E-mails are infinitely less intrusive than phone calls and if they're approached respectfully and politely, most successful people appreciate the opportunity to share what they've learned. Remember, when the pupil is ready the teacher will appear. So get ready.

While finding a mentor is essential to leadership mastery, especially at the beginning of your career, being a mentor is also hugely rewarding and beneficial as time moves along. So volunteer to teach a class in your field of expertise. Get involved with the schools you attended. Get your name out into the world by writing articles or giving talks. By doing so, you'll make it easier for anyone who needs a mentor to find you. There are also many organizations devoted to bringing potential mentors and mentored together. Once again, the World Wide Web is a great way to research this.

Become Interested in Others

There are an almost infinite number of ways to say, "I care about the community and the people in it, and I want to give my time to help." This isn't just altruism. As a leader and mentor there's a great deal in it for you. Dale Carnegie understood this very well. He wrote, "If you want others to like you, if you want to help others, if you want them to achieve success just as you want success for yourself, keep this principle in mind. Become sincerely interested in other people." And there's no doubt that Dale Carnegie practiced what he preached.

When J. Oliver Crom, past president of Dale Carnegie & Associates, first met Dale Carnegie, he wasn't sure what to expect. "Mr. Carnegie, I'm pleased to meet you," Mr. Crom said. "Oh, please call me Dale," came the reply. "Mr. Carnegie sounds so formal. I understand you were born in Alliance, Nebraska. Is that correct?" "Well, yes," said Crom, somewhat taken aback. "Then tell me," Dale Carnegie inquired, "do the same wonderful people live in Alliance that lived there so many years ago when I used to sell in that territory? Please tell me more about the people out there and please tell me more about yourself. It will help me, and perhaps it will help you also."

As you might expect, this meant a lot to the young man from Nebraska. It's simply a fact of human nature that people do best personally and professionally when they know that someone of goodwill is paying attention, when they know that person cares about them, and when they know that person is ready to help if need be. Conversely, if you feel like you're living in a vacuum, you're not going to be motivated to live at your best. If the Super Bowl were played in an empty stadium, there might still be a game, but the level of intensity and performance would certainly be very different.

Mentoring is a way of taking your daily challenges out of the empty stadium and into the big game. For a leader, finding a mentor and being a mentor is not just an option or a sidelight, it's an essential component of peak performance.

ADMIRATION AND LIKABILITY:
CAN YOU BE A MENTOR?

Although an admired person may not always be likable, in an organizational setting, people respect and appreciate a noble executive who takes on responsibility for difficult decisions and their thorny consequences. Managers who run after fame and only claim glory are usually detected early on and kicked out sooner or later.

While a likable person may be scared to share his real thoughts and be an active group thinker, natural-born leaders will share their thoughts and are honest about the pros and cons of an issue. People admire leaders not only for their thoughtful leadership, but also their rigor and balanced care.

One must realize that people admire brave leaders who do not simply try to cover their tracks, but think about the real benefits of their decisions for the company. Selfish corporate managers who try to put their careers and their gain ahead of the corporate objectives are weeded out and disgraced over time.

Some executives are more willing than others to take responsibility for failures and take the difficult steps to alleviate the situation. Some simply flee and shift the blame. The former type make good mentors. The others may be in need of mentors themselves.

Optimize the Problems

It occasionally happens that the CEO of a company will need to take the heat for actions by subordinates that he or she was entirely unaware of. This has been the case in a number of corporate meltdowns over the years. Even if the leader of a company is not personally involved, he or she must accept responsibility and address the need to implement changes. This captain of the ship mentality is the way to gain the esteem and respect of colleagues and employees. This is what winning admiration in the workplace really means.

Can anyone really like you? Can anyone really learn from you? Can you have one without the other?

You Really Like Me. Don't You?

The decision to fire colleagues and take responsibility for someone else's failure is difficult. But the willingness to improve the situation and put your own neck on the line is a noble decision that many executives would simply prefer to avoid. Most would throw in the towel, disappear, and reappear a few years later, right before another major expensive scandal.

The bottom line is that people seek mentors (and leaders) who are honest and bold and adhere to higher levels of integrity. Shareholders and employees have an easier time swallowing unpleasant surprises relayed by eloquent and congenial managers. Well-explained complex projects championed by admired executives enjoy greater buy-in from stakeholders than those pushed by arrogant and obnoxious officers.

Not-Nice Guys Finish Last

Forget the popular misleading belief about "nice guys." Bad guys are the ones who finish last and early.

Look back at the "dot bomb" hype, the Enron collapse, and the even more recent mortgage and credit crisis. Life is a real boomerang, and people who enjoy being ruthless and make regular folks feel worthless end up tasting their own medicine down the road.

Remember "Chainsaw" Al Dunlap at Sunbeam? You may not, which should tell you something already. After he cut payroll as if there were no tomorrow, shareholders realized that the promised goods wouldn't be delivered, and he was just as quickly out the door. *Time* magazine wrote in 1998: "Sunbeam's tumbling stock price and the problems behind it spurred the company's board to

'Dunlap' the man whose name means to lay off." How ironic! And what about the executives of Bear Stearns, Lehman, AIG, and all the rest?

This is not advice to let people walk all over you. Simply avoid being cruel and insensitive to the personal implications of business decisions. It's a small world, so make sure you can sleep at night without feeling haunted by guilt.

Another thing is quite sure: Congeniality is definitely a success factor. Business leaders with daunting projects to deliver (while facing difficult economic times) had better remember that their biggest allies are the people who have to deliver the anticipated results and those who bear the brunt of the decisions made in the conference room.

Success is derived by how well these people are motivated and mentored by the executive's bold character and compassion for those who are impacted by these executive decisions. Let's not forget that.

A FINAL POINT ON MENTORING

One final point about mentoring deserves your close attention: Believe it or not, you don't have to choose your mentors from people you're able to meet or contact, or even from people who are alive. As a leader you should learn to imagine and internalize the wisdom of individuals you admire regardless of when they lived or what language they spoke. If you're faced with pressing financial questions, read a biography of someone like Andrew Carnegie or Henry Ford.

Find out what strategies and tactics helped these people rise from humble beginnings to the pinnacle of financial success. Then once you've learned the facts about your historical mentors, imagine what they would actually say if you were to ask them for advice about your situation. This can literally become a form of meditation, one in which you close your eyes and imagine you're conducting a face-to-face interview with a mentor from the past.

The action steps at the end of this chapter have more information about how to go about this. The first step, though, is realizing that literally anyone can be your mentor, provided you take the time to learn the facts about their lives and the tools they used to achieve their success.

ACTION STEPS

1. In creating your goals, it's most useful to work backward. In other words, begin with very long-term objectives. Make a list of at least five goals that you would like to achieve by the end of your life. Try to make them as specific as possible. For example, don't just write that you want to travel. List the specific destinations. Then take some time and identify at least five of your medium-term goals (taking two to ten years to accomplish), and five of your short-term goals (requiring less than two years to achieve). Once you've done this, set deadlines for each, and begin acting on them. Remember, success happens one step at a time.

2. Do a life review, and take note of any mentors who have positively affected you. Write their names down, along with what accomplishments you made in response to their encouragement. Then if you haven't already, take some time to call or write to them, letting them know how much they affected your life. Expressing gratitude is a powerful way to attract even greater things into your life.

3. Take some time to meditate on a mentor. Find a comfortable place where you can sit for at least fifteen minutes undisturbed. You may wish to play some quiet, soothing music, or simply sit in silence. To start, make a list of the criteria that you are looking for in a mentor. Then set the

intention to connect with that perfect mentor. Take some slow deep breaths and quiet your mind. Sit in the stillness until names, faces, images, or ideas begin to come to mind. If they do not, then revisit your list of criteria and quiet yourself again. If you do not get an immediate image, do not be concerned. Within the week someone will come to mind. Again, if not, you may wish to do some research on the Web or by reading biographies and autobiographies. Trust that your commitment to finding a mentor will be enough to steer you in the right direction.

4. Think about people in your life with whom you feel a connection and whom you would be honored to mentor. Record these names and write down ways in which you can reach out to them and begin the process.

Don't limit expressions of interest to the seemingly important people in your life. The chances are they already get enough attention.

—Dale Carnegie

CHAPTER 5

The Hallmarks of Leadership Talent

D id you ever stop to think that a dog is one of the only animals that does not have to work for a living? A hen has to lay eggs, a cow has to give milk, and a canary has to sing. But a dog makes his living by giving you nothing but love. They are the light and joy in many people's lives. As companions, they are always so interested in you, and love you unconditionally. No matter what your mood, or how you are approaching life, your dog is always sure to greet you with leaps of joy and barks of sheer ecstasy just to see you.

Dogs never read books on psychology. They don't need to. They know by some divine instinct that you can make more friends in two months by becoming genuinely interested in other people than you can in two years by trying to get other people interested in you. This truism bears repeating: You can make more friends in two months by becoming interested in other people than you can in two years by trying to get other people interested in you.

Yet we all know people who go through life trying to get other people interested in them. Of course it doesn't work. People are not interested in you. They're not interested in me. They're interested in themselves.

The subject we will discuss in this chapter is how to recognize talent not only in other people, but first and foremost in yourself. These are characteristics that true leaders bring to anything they do, whether it's a particular task, a certain job title, an organization, or even a family.

COMMUNICATE!

A leader talks like a leader. They don't all talk the same way, but all leaders have certain communication skills that set them apart from other team members. They communicate their competence in a highly effective way. When good leaders speak, the troops understand what they are saying and are ready to act on their ideas.

People who can express themselves well are increasingly rare, which makes good communication skills all the more valuable. You are evaluated not only by what you say, but by how you say it. When you lead a meeting, for example, you must be able to present your ideas clearly and get them right the first time. Moreover, be aware that over and above the content of what you are saying, you are the message. If team members leave the meeting with a positive impression of you as a human being, it will strengthen the information you tried to communicate, especially if you did so in a powerful manner.

Sometimes it's useful to think of communication as a game. To be successful in any game, you first need to learn how to play. In other words, what are the rules?

The rules of good communication are a lot like the rules of good driving. First and foremost, there's the issue of who's behind the wheel. When you're speaking by yourself in front of a group, it's as if you were behind the wheel of a car full of people, or maybe even a bus. You're the one with your foot on the gas pedal or the brake. You're in charge and there's not much your passengers can do about it. Still, it's in your best interests to make the ride as enjoyable as possible. So don't go too fast or too slow. Don't make the journey take any longer than it has to. And if you decide to take the scenic route, make sure it's really scenic!

A one-on-one conversation is more like driving though the city alone in your car. The other drivers are like your conversation partner. You've got to be aware of their presence and their needs, just as you're aware of your own. You need to halt at stop signs and give up the right of way when appropriate. You can't just act as if no one else is there. People who talk nonstop are like speeding road hogs. But going too slow isn't good either. Driving safely and talking effectively require a combination of self-awareness and consideration of others around you. Perhaps unfortunately, people don't need a license to start talking.

Once you know the rules of oral communication—and begin to obey them—you must tap into three basic resources for becoming truly proficient. These are not just oratorical techniques. They're fundamental principles of character. They're the underlying foundation of everything you say.

The first principle is competence. A really competent leader should be capable of doing literally every job in the organization. You can't just be a marketing expert, you must also know about finance and operations and everything else. There's nothing more embarrassing than the head of an automotive company who doesn't know how to check the oil in a car, or a software executive who can't attach a file to an e-mail.

The second principle is clarity. Before you can communicate your vision, it has to exist very clearly in your mind. Strong leaders have clear visions of where their company and their industry are heading. On an even larger scale, they can see where the economy as a whole is heading and guide their company accordingly.

Creating a vision and direction for an organization is not done in a vacuum. Leaders must know the historical trends, the current situation, and what the future is most likely to hold.

Once the principles of competence and clarity are in place, the real process of communication can take place. Often the ideas and visions of a leader are new, clear but complex, and not necessarily easy to communicate. However, if the leader and his company are to be successful, he or she must learn to convey the vision.

Competence, clarity, and communication—three C's. Talented leaders have naturally mastered these. Less talented leaders can also master them through hard work and experience. The key lesson is, leaders know how to move what's in their heads (and hearts) into every member of their teams.

Jeff Winston Wins Over a Formidable Opponent

Jeff Winston's experience has made him something of an expert in all these areas. Ten years ago he was fresh out of college when he appeared for an interview at one of the country's leading news-magazines. He was hired, and during the decade he spent at the magazine he wore many hats. First he was a fact-checker, then a researcher, then a reporter, and finally a senior editor. Now Jeff has been named managing editor at a new publication in the high-technology field. It's a great opportunity for offering leadership in a new direction.

Jeff is proud of his new position but he also knows he's earned it. Over the past ten years he's climbed every rung of the ladder. When he was first appointed to a senior editorial position at the news magazine, Jeff found most of his colleagues were very supportive and encouraging. However, he felt some tension in his relationship with one of the editors, who now reported to him, a man whom he himself had once worked for during his early years at the magazine. As Jeff recalls, he was a very talented writer and editor but never achieved the top positions at the magazine that he felt he deserved.

"When I was given one of those positions he became convinced it was because of politics rather than real ability on my part. He didn't confront me directly but several other people told me what he thought." Jeff tried not to let this bother him but he did feel some anger toward the other editor. The more he thought about it, however, the more he realized that any real fault probably lay within himself.

If the other man did not consider Jeff worthy of the promotion, it could only be because he did not recognize Jeff's real talent. But it wasn't really his responsibility to recognize Jeff's talent. Instead it was Jeff's responsibility to make his talent recognizable and beyond question. With this in the back of his mind, Jeff worked hard in his new position as senior editor. He helped find and develop story ideas. He spent many hours talking with the writers, department editors, and art directors. He took a sincere interest in all the diverse editorial content that was his responsibility, including medicine, media, religion, and lifestyle. Although it wasn't exactly easy, he made a special effort to work well with the man who had questioned his ability.

Then one day after Jeff had been a senior editor for about six months, the editor with whom he had the problem walked into his office. He was an older man who had acquired real seniority at the magazine and he wasn't afraid to exert it, regardless of his job title. So he simply strolled into Jeff's office late one afternoon and occupied the chair in front of Jeff's desk.

"Jeff, I have to tell you something," he said in a low voice. "When you got this job I was totally against it. I thought you were too young, that you lacked experience, and that it was all happening because you went to an Ivy League school. But I've really been impressed by the interest you've shown in developing content in the writers, and in the departments' editors, including myself. I've worked with a lot of other senior editors and all of them were just interested in using this as a stepping-stone to the next level. It's clear to me, though, that you're really committed to this job. You show that commitment every day and you've got talent too."

Today in his new position at the business magazine, Jeff can look back on that encounter with some insight. He can see the problem that led up to it, and he can also see how his efforts avoided a potentially difficult situation. You have to take people seriously in order for them to take you seriously, he says. Whether you're coming in off the street for an interview or moving into a new executive position, you have to show that you're meeting everyone on an equal playing field. If you can do that, the talents you have will show through without anyone's emotions getting in the way.

EXPRESS INTEREST IN OTHERS

This is a basic principle of the Dale Carnegie philosophy. Expressing interest in others is the best way to make them interested in you. People can't help responding to people who are sincerely interested in them. This is the all-important principle that leaders should look for in others and that they themselves should express. Taking genuine interest is the one basic talent that makes all other talents possible. When you have it, there's no limit to how far you can move ahead. When you don't have it, it's unlikely any of your other abilities will be recognized.

There are many different ways of expressing interest in people and most of them require nothing more than a bit of focused attention. And the higher up you go on the leadership ladder the more important these habits become. Showing you care about people is not a sign of weakness or lack of authority in a leader. On the contrary, it is evidence of true leadership talent. It is proof that you deserve to be where you are.

It can be as simple as using a pleasant voice on the telephone, a voice that says "I'm happy to hear from you." When you meet people in person, greet them with genuine pleasure. Smile, learn their names, remember them, and make sure you spell and pronounce them correctly. Upon meeting a new person, write this information down as soon as possible. Also be aware when someone shows this kind of thoughtfulness toward you. When they do, they're not just being polite; they're showing the potential to be a leader. Above all, don't limit these expressions of interest to so-called important people.

For one thing, they probably get quite a bit of attention already. For another thing, who is important today is very likely to change by tomorrow or the day after. Don't forget the assistants, receptionists, messengers, and all the other individuals who keep an organization running. Once again, when you see someone else showing this kind of consideration, keep an eye on him or her. They may be ready for greater responsibilities.

The chief operating officer of a food services corporation in Minnesota had an interesting experience in this regard. He was in the company cafeteria when he happened to overhear a conversation between a mid-level manager and one of the department heads. It seemed that the manager had been going through a difficult period in his life and it was beginning to affect his work. The department head was listening carefully, just letting the other man express his feelings to the fullest extent possible. Then the department head made some very practical and useful suggestions while also making it clear he was concerned on a personal level.

Based on this conversation, the chief operating officer chose the department head to handle a very sensitive negotiation that was beginning with an important new customer. It was a definite step up for the department head. It was also a chance for the company to make use of talents that might not show up in a résumé or an annual review. Such displays of interest are the fundamental building blocks of successful relationships, both personal and professional. They are the moments that say, "You are important to me. I'm interested, I want to know more, and I care." Most people in this world want to experience that, and leadership masters make sure they do.

Having Concern for Others Keeps You Positive

Once you start this process it will quickly become a natural part of your leadership style. Before you know it, by expressing interest, you will naturally become more interested in the people around you. What's more, genuine interest in others is one of the best ways to move beyond any worries or concerns that may be troubling you personally. The more you stay focused on other people, the fewer negative thoughts you'll have.

Bestselling author Harvey Mackay had a long career in the envelope business. That's where he learned many of the lessons that have made his books and articles so insightful. Mackay recalls a salesman whom he never regarded as particularly dynamic or successful despite the man's many years of experience at his company. On one occasion, though, Mackay says, "I remember him telling me that one of his buyers had just welcomed a new baby girl into his family. So the salesman went down and bought a gift. But not for the new baby; it was for her older brother, a little boy of three who might be feeling some pangs of jealousy about now."

Mackay continues, "That one very thoughtful and creative gesture stuck with me right away. All of a sudden I didn't think of him as an average employee anymore. Now he's one of our key regional sales managers."

EFFECTIVE LEADERSHIP TAKES MORE THAN GOOD PERFORMANCE

Conversely, a senior vice president at Bank of America learned the hard way about the importance of taking a genuine interest in others. He had gotten an impressively fast start at an investment firm after graduating from college in the late 1980s. Much sooner than he had ever expected, he had a large apartment in San Francisco and a Mercedes in the driveway. "I thought I had it all and I let people know that I thought so," he says today. "I had a real attitude but just as the recession was approaching in 1990, my boss called me into his office and said I was going to be terminated.

"I was in total shock and I pointed out all the good work I had done for the firm, but my boss just shook his head," recalls the executive. "'It's not a matter of numbers,' the boss said. 'That's performance, but we're not looking just for performance. We need leadership talent. People just don't like working with you. I'm afraid we're going to have to part company.' It hit me like a rock," says the executive. "I considered myself Mr. Success and now I was getting fired and the recession was just getting under way. It took a full year before I found another job."

An even more dramatic story comes from a direct-marketing executive who had his own nationwide organization. "I had forty offices across the country and in Canada," he says. "I was constantly in touch with my people in the various markets and I liked to make them jump through hoops. Sometimes I'd tell a guy in Atlanta that he was going to have to move to Boston or I'd tell the guy in Boston that he should start looking for housing in Phoenix. I was on an incredible power trip."

Until one day there was an express mail delivery of forty envelopes. Inside each envelope there was a set of keys. "My entire company had gotten together and quit on me at one time. I was literally out of business. It took me years to get back on my feet, but I'm actually grateful for what happened. I had it coming, and believe me, it will never happen again."

ACTION STEPS

1. Make a list of five people with whom you are in regular contact in your professional life. They may be colleagues, customers, suppliers, or perhaps even competitors. You may never have thought of these people as particularly gifted, but each one of them has very special and unique qualities.

Leadership masters know this, and they are determined to develop the true natural strengths of everyone around them. So after each name, write at least three of the strongest unique talents in each of the individuals.

2. Now after looking at the talents that you see in others, list five of your natural strengths. After each one, describe a specific occasion when you have put this talent to use. You may not even be aware of a special gift that you have. By focusing on particular strengths in which you have performed well, however, you'll begin to gain awareness of similar opportunities as they arise.

3. The two accounts at the end of this chapter are hard reminders of times when good performance is clearly not all that is required. Do you have a similar situation in which your own self-interest overshadowed your interest in others, and actually impeded your chance to excel in a particular situation? If so, write about it, and then write a list of things you could have done to potentially shift that outcome. While hindsight is twenty-twenty, it is useful to review past errors to pave the way to improvement.

The best way to get someone excited about an idea is to be excited yourself. And to show it.

—Dale Carnegie

CHAPTER 6

The Four Qualities of Leadership Masters

While expressing sincere interest in other people is a core talent of leadership mastery, this talent can show itself in many specific ways at any point in your career. To start, there are certain very clear traits by which leadership masters identify themselves and engage others, and it doesn't matter whether they're waiting in an outer office for a job interview or sitting behind a desk in an executive suite. These qualities are optimism, cheerfulness, creativity, and the ability to overcome setbacks. We'll look at these qualities one by one during the rest of this chapter, and we'll offer suggestions for making them part of your personal leadership style.

OPTIMISM

After a sincere interest in others, optimism is the most basic element of leadership talent. This is hardly a new insight, and in fact it was the subject of a bestselling book by the psychologist Martin Seligman. In his book *Learned Optimism*, Seligman showed that a high percentage of successful individuals shared one key characteristic: the belief that things would turn out well. This was more important than education, business connections, or financial resources. Interestingly, it was even more important than being right. Pessimists may be correct at times in thinking that endeavors will end badly, but that accuracy about the future only steers them toward inactivity in the present.

Optimists on the other hand refuse to take no for an answer. They bounce back. When things go wrong they don't believe that they do because this is how the universe is constructed. Instead they see it as a temporary glitch. Optimism was hard to come by in the early '80s, when Thomas J. Peters and Robert H. Waterman were beginning work on their book *In Search of Excellence.* American business was taking a beating from competition around the world and it was a general perception that perhaps our best days were behind us.

For Peters and Waterman, however, this was a golden opportunity to take advantage of the power of optimism. Plenty of writers and journalists were busy telling us how bad things were. *In Search of Excellence,* however, focused on what we were doing right. The authors sought out the most successful American companies in a variety of industries and carefully documented the steps those companies followed toward success. As it turned out, the publisher of *In Search of Excellence* was less optimistic than either the book's subjects or its authors. The first printing would be only 10,000 copies, so small that it would justify little advertising or promotion by the publisher.

Yet Peters and Waterman were optimists about their book and they also showed real leadership mastery in the solution they found for this problem. If only 10,000 books were going to be printed, the authors decided that they would just have to make 15,000 Xerox copies of the manuscript and give them away. That's exactly what happened, despite the strenuous objections of the publisher.

The book ended up becoming one of the best-selling business books of all time. Of course, this was precisely because Peters and

Waterman believed in it and were willing to act on their optimistic belief.

Optimism Is a Conscious Choice

An electronics dealer in Milwaukee recalls talking to a colleague who was concerned that a rival business was opening across the street. As they talked, the more experienced man made some interesting points. First, it would take the new dealer at least six months to open his doors. Second, a successful, established business has a tremendous advantage and the first store had been just that for more than ten years. There was a lot of loyalty and goodwill already in place.

So why was the dealer so concerned that the sky was falling? It wasn't reality-based insight. It was just plain and simple pessimism, and it was a perfect example of someone leading himself in the wrong direction. Leadership masters think, know, and feel that they're going to get the job. They're going to receive the promotion. They're going to close the deal and they're going to be more successful than last year, but not as successful as they will be next year. Is that the positive approach you bring to every area of your life? If not, please turn some attention to it and be optimistic that your attitude will change.

CHEERFULNESS

Cheerfulness is a natural companion of optimism and deserves some discussion in its own right. For reasons that may not be exactly clear, people often associate grave or even sad mannerisms with intelligence. Perhaps they assume that someone who seems serious or concerned must know something we don't. In any case, the connection between melancholy and wisdom is unfortunate and unproductive, and it is not shared by people in all parts of the world.

In China, for example, happiness is associated with intelligence and tenacity, particularly as people mature. A person who has faced life's trials and retains the ability to be happy must be a strong person, a survivor, someone qualified to lead. In fact, leadership masters make it their business to communicate cheerfulness to everyone in their personal and professional lives.

The importance of this was made very clear in an encounter between the CEO of a successful insurance company and a manager in his organization. At a private meeting in the office the younger man seemed concerned and even glum. "What's the trouble?" asked the head of the company. "Is there a problem?" "Well, sir, I'm afraid there is," said the manager. "Sales figures for this quarter are down, way down." He looked hesitantly toward the CEO, not at all sure what to expect. To his surprise the man looked perfectly composed and cheerful. "That's excellent," he declared. "That's really excellent, I'm very pleased." The manager looked puzzled. "But how can it be excellent? I just told you the sales figures are way down and you seem happy about it." "That's right, I am happy," said the CEO. "For one thing I've heard this kind of news before and it's never been more than a temporary problem. As a matter of fact, it usually provides an opportunity for changes that pay off big in the long run. But even more important, it's a matter of personal discipline for me to always react cheerfully to bad news, even if I can't find the silver lining in the cloud right at the moment, I know that a good-natured response maximizes my chances of finding it as soon as possible. I know it's there, and I know it will make me stronger and more successful over time, so what's not to be happy about?"

George Cheerfully Promises and Delivers

Take the example of George, one of the most successful, energetic, and fun-loving executives in America. George has a net worth of more than a billion dollars as CEO and president of a manufacturer of computer components. Shortly after George started his career with the computer manufacturing company, he met with senior-level executives of a huge buyer of computer components. During this meeting, the senior-level executives told George they would never buy components from a start-up organization that had not yet established credibility.

George broke into a big smile. Then he asked about the capabilities of the technology the large company was currently using. Upon hearing the answer, the entrepreneur's grin grew even wider and he promised that within a year he would return with a component at least ten times more powerful than the one they just described, which is exactly what happened.

Leadership masters are not only prepared to do whatever it takes, they're happy about doing it and rise to the challenge.

All of us are going to face ups and downs and some of them will be quite severe, but a true leader's talent is the ability to behave positively, even when things seem to be going wrong. In short, being glum is not a sign of intelligence, and being cheerful in the face of adversity is certainly not an indicator of ignorance. On the contrary, it's a sign of leadership mastery.

CREATIVITY

A third aspect of leadership talent is creativity. We can define creativity as the ability to make something of value out of something of lesser value. To go even further, it's the ability to make something of value out of nothing at all. So if someone is angry and insults you, turning their anger to friendship could be considered a creative act. Animosity between two people is unlikely to produce anything positive, but friends working together can bring about miracles.

A different form of creativity takes place when a dream is turned into a reality, when a thought becomes a tangible object that can benefit yourself or perhaps the world. Perhaps this really is the ultimate creative expression since wishes, thoughts, and dreams are at the foundation of all reality.

A Mouse Becomes a Famous Icon

Let's look for a moment at how the creative process manifested itself in one of the true founders of contemporary popular culture. As with any thought or any dream, the origins are difficult to pinpoint either on a map, or a calendar, or within the mind of the dreamer. According to one story, a young artist named Walter E. Disney found a family of mice in his studio and he eventually decided to make them into cartoon characters. Another story tells how Disney was kept awake on an overnight train trip by the creaking of the woodwork in his compartment. It sounded to him like a chorus of mice, and in that second Mickey Mouse came into being. No one really knows the truth, but there is no doubt of one thing. Late in life, after the building of Disneyland and the production of dozens of successful films, Walt Disney liked to remind people that a mouse started it all.

What he really meant, of course, was that it came from the idea of a mouse. And if ever there was a case of nothing turning into something, it was the idea of a mouse turning into a multibillion-dollar business empire. Perhaps even the word *talent* does not do justice to that phenomenon. It would have to be called genius.

THE ABILITY TO OVERCOME SETBACKS

Walt Disney's life also illuminates a fourth aspect of leadership aptitude. This is resilience, or the capacity to rebound from setbacks and disappointments (or in Disney's case, flat-out failures). Burdened with huge debts after the failure of his Laugh-O-Gram animation company in Kansas City, Walt Disney moved to California and looked for a job. He couldn't find one, but he didn't quit. Instead he started a new film company with his older brother Roy.

Their first two animated films were commercially unsuccessful and Walt Disney even lost the rights to the second one because of a naïve business decision. Then came the family of mice in the studio, and/or the squeaky woodwork on the train. Mickey Mouse came into being, or not quite. Disney originally wanted to name him Mortimer but his wife talked him out of it. So maybe she was the real creator. In any case, Walt Disney created something that led millions of people over several generations to follow where his dreams led. This is leadership mastery of a unique kind, especially since the followers had so much fun. Taking a sincere interest in others, optimism, cheerfulness, creativity, and the ability to transcend disappointment or even failure. These are hallmarks of leadership talent. Learn to recognize them in people. Look for them in yourself, and if you find them lacking, do everything in your power to develop them, starting today.

THE LEADER SETS THE TONE

Effective leaders set the tone for the entire organization. It's not a matter of knowing more than everyone else. There are plenty of leaders who aren't the biggest experts in their companies. But it does mean working hard, something anyone can do. Be the first person to arrive at the workplace and be the last one to leave. If you can do that, you'll already be light years ahead of most managers in the respect you'll gain from your team members. Apply the same principle to all your routine activities. If you expect your sales force to make 50 calls each day, make 100 calls yourself. It's not rocket science. It's just basic "lead by example" management.

No one can really discredit leaders who are the hardest-working individuals in their organizations. And very few people can match their results. Hard work always beats lazy talent, and talented hard work trumps everything. So set your alarm clock. Set it for early.

SPEAK SOFTLY (AND AS LITTLE AS POSSIBLE)

Often the best way to exercise authority is simply to keep your mouth shut. Many people have the misconception that the smartest guy in the room is the one who does all the talking. Whoever hogs the microphone must be the leader, right? Well, no. The real leader is not the individual who says the most. It's the person who needs to say the least,

This is especially true in meetings and presentations. When you're in a leadership position and you want to project an image of confidence and maturity, focus intently on what others are saying but keep silent yourself. Let everyone else run out of gas. Then, when you do speak, your words will carry maximum authority. Instead of rushing into decisions and pronouncements, absorb as much information as possible. It's amazing how many mistakes you won't make if you spend more time listening than speaking.

Often finding the best solution to a problem means spending a great deal of time listening to other people's points of view before forming your own. If you can, have the last word in the meeting after you've collected as much information as possible, because it's an effective way to project leadership.

In everyday conversation, most people can't wait to share their points of view on a dozen topics—movies, sports, music, food, whatever. But in everyday conversation choosing our words very carefully isn't too important, and the consequences of being wrong about the outcome of a ball game are very minor. But when you're in a leadership role in the business world, the ground rules change significantly.

Here's another common misconception. Sometimes people confuse the relationship between questions and answers. When a leader asks a lot of questions, that doesn't mean he or she is uncertain or confused. On the contrary, leaders who ask questions do so because they intend to make the best decision possible and they need information to make that happen. The best leaders learn to ask lots of questions to get to the root of problems. They know how to dig. The majority of leadership decisions actually become obvious once a manager gets enough facts about the situation. On the other hand, too many problems go unsolved because the answers seem more obvious than they really are.

For example, if a project is behind schedule and no one seems to know why, don't just ask, "Who's responsible for this?" Trace the whole sequence of events. See if there's a larger problem behind the work not getting done. Many underlying issues are overlooked by managers who are unwilling or unable to ask the deeper questions.

Once you've got the required information, act boldly. Effective leaders make confident decisions. Excessive caution is a bad way to enhance the importance of your decision and your authority as a leader.

This doesn't mean that you can't ever change your mind. But if you do, be sure to make the changes few and far between and only in the most demanding circumstances. When leaders backtrack, there's always a ripple effect. Because you've questioned your earlier decision, your team members may question your next one too.

Especially if you're newly promoted or if you've just joined a new organization, don't worry if you sometimes have to pretend you know what you're doing. Everyone has done that. To a great extent leadership is a trial by fire. Books and classes can certainly help, but true leadership is a skill that's acquired by experience. It's a matter of knowing how to communicate well and to project confidence in your own abilities. It takes practice!

JOSEPHINE CARNEGIE'S STORY

Josephine Carnegie, Dale Carnegie's niece, had come to New York to be Dale Carnegie's secretary. She was nineteen, had graduated from high school three years previously, and her business experience was a trifle more than zero. She became one of the most proficient secretaries he knew, but in the beginning she was ripe for improvement. One day when he started to criticize her, he said to himself, "Now just a minute, Dale Carnegie, just a minute. You're twice as old as Josephine. You've had ten thousand times as much business experience. How can you possibly expect her to have your viewpoint, your judgment, and your initiative? What were you doing at nineteen? Remember the silly mistakes and blunders you made? Remember the time you did this and that?" After thinking the matter over honestly and impartially, he concluded that Josephine's batting average at nineteen was better than his had been, and that wasn't paying Josephine much of a compliment. So after that realization, when he wanted to call Josephine's attention to a mistake, he'd begin by saying, "You've made a mistake, Josephine, but the Lord knows it's no worse than many I've made. You were not born with judgment. That comes only with experience, and you are better than I was at your age. I've been guilty of so many stupid, silly things myself. I have very little inclination to criticize you or anyone, but don't you think it would have been wiser if you had done so and so?" It isn't nearly so difficult to listen to a recital of your faults if the person criticizing begins by humbly admitting that he too is far from impeccable.

ACTION STEPS

1. List three concerns that you face presently, personally or professionally. How do you see these concerns being resolved? For each item, write an optimistic description of how this might occur, and then take that description to heart. Lead yourself in that direction. Make the best possible result the one that actually happens!

2. List the names of three of the most cheerful people you know. Briefly describe an incident in which their

cheerfulness was especially evident. Then make note of what you can learn from each, and how you can incorporate cheerfulness into at least two challenges that you are currently facing in your life.

3. In this chapter we spoke of Walt Disney. His creativity and resilience were remarkable. When have you behaved with admirable resilience?

4. What opportunities exist right now for you to exhibit the four traits of leadership mastery? What can you do today to move in this direction?

There is one longing almost as deep and imperious as the desire for food or sleep. It is the desire to be great. It is the desire to be important.

—Dale Carnegie

CHAPTER 7

Embracing Risk

DANCOFF'S FORMULA

More than fifty years ago an article by a scientist named Sidney Dancoff appeared in a leading physics journal. Although Dancoff had worked on many projects in nuclear physics, including the building of the first atomic bomb, he had more recently turned his attention to biophysics (the intersection of biology and physical science). In his article, Sidney Dancoff proposed a formula that was both simple and profound. Although it was intended to describe biological processes at the microscopic level, the formula had obvious relevance to all areas of our lives.

It's one of those ideas that causes you say to yourself, "Hey, why didn't I think of that"? Dancoff's formula, known as the principle of maximum error, can be stated as follows: Optimum development occurs when an organism makes the maximum number of mistakes consistent with survival. In other words, the more mistakes you make, the closer you become to your best possible self, provided the mistakes don't kill you. So it would seem that nonfatal mistakes are not things to avoid. In fact, they should actually be sought out by people who want to evolve toward their full potential. The formula doesn't say, of course, that the mistakes will be painless. It doesn't say they won't cost you money, or that you won't lose sleep at night. It does say, however, that if you keep trying, you will get better. This is certainly true at the biological level (the original focus of the formula), but is perhaps also true emotionally and even spiritually. At least that's what a leadership master would say, because leadership masters have often made a lot of mistakes in their lives. They made mistakes because, like all leaders, they embrace risk. They see risk as a basic requirement for gain; not only for their financial or material gain, but also for their growth as leaders and as human beings.

A REAL ESTATE MAVERICK LOOKING FOR RISK

One of the most successful real estate developers in America was famous for asking a few straightforward questions whenever someone came to him with a proposal. Before anything else was even said, the developer always inquired, "How much could I lose in this deal? How badly can I get hurt? What is the ratio of risk to possible reward?" If there was no risk, the developer never needed to hear any more. He wasn't interested because he knew, as the saying goes, that there really is no such thing as a free lunch.

If a deal offered little chance for a big payoff, it wasn't worth his time or money. If it seemed to have low risk but the promise of significant gain, he knew there must be something wrong. In his eyes, in the real world of business, things simply don't work that way, although people would tell him otherwise.

Asking about the risk was the best way to cut to the chase. If the developer learned he could get wiped out, his attention was immediately aroused. He saw the possibility of getting wiped out as a precondition for the possibility of a huge success. This real estate developer applied a simple principle when he interviewed prospects for executive positions in his company. As he described it, "Most people try to make themselves look good. They do that by talking about all the great successes they've had. So they're quite surprised when I ask to hear about their biggest failures, and they'd better have some good ones if they expect to join our organization. If a person has never failed, it tells me they've never taken any risks, and that's a bad sign. An absence of defeat also means you've never had to recover from anything. You've never had to pull yourself up off the ground and get back into the game. I don't need people like that. We take a lot of risks around here and sometimes we get hurt. When that happens, I need executives who can lead us back from misfortune because they've led themselves back before."

LOU NOTO UNDERSTOOD POSITIVE RISK-TAKING

Lucio A. Noto, the former chairman and CEO of Mobil Corporation, is another leader who has thought a great deal about the role of risk in a successful organization. When Mobil's merger with Exxon was announced in 1998, one of the world's largest corporations came into being. Lou Noto had been with Mobil for more than thirty years. Many other employees had looked at their careers with the oil company as a cradle-to-grave proposition, but the merger made layoffs and early retirements unavoidable.

While he had to let almost five thousand workers go, he did not have to dismiss as many as at other large companies did during the heyday of downsizing. This counted for about 7 percent of the total workforce. In its aftermath, the CEO was concerned that the sixty-two thousand people who remained would want to play it safe to protect their jobs. That seemed like a disastrous possibility to Lou Noto, who understood the positive aspects of risk-taking. As he described it in an interview, the company was becoming totally success oriented without understanding everything that success really required. It was as if people were doing projects that cost a thousand dollars to net a fifty-dollar return.

True, there was minimal risk, but sometimes even low-risk endeavors don't work out. So where was the logic? What was needed were thousand-dollar projects that had at least a reasonable chance of making ten thousand or even a hundred thousand. And if there was also a chance of failure, Mobil should be eager to pay that price.

If you expect people to develop into leaders, you can't tell them they'll be fired if they don't hit a home run every time they swing the bat. If you want to become a leadership master, you've got to get used to swinging that bat yourself and you've got to love swinging for the fences.

RISK-TAKERS OPEN THEMSELVES
TO OPPORTUNITY

As the late billionaire John Paul Getty once wrote, there are one hundred people seeking security for every person willing to risk his fortune. "Here's how I look at it," said a successful screenwriter in Los Angeles. "For me, success means access to opportunity. If I can get to a point where I've got a real chance to close a big sale, I think I've already won. Now I'm able to take my shot, and if it doesn't go in the basket, maybe the next one will. But I never beat myself up for missing or for taking the risk of putting myself on the line."

He pointed to a shelf of unproduced screenplays. "Each one of those took me at least six months to write. Each one represents a big investment in time and effort, a risk that didn't pay off financially because none of them sold. But I think of them as successes because they gave me access to opportunity. They opened it up for the ones that did sell, and the money I got for them more than justifies the expense of the others."

This is the kind of proactive approach to risk that a leadership master needs to develop. When you're faced with a risky situation, don't feel you have to be a daredevil. If there's a probable chance of success, however, train yourself to focus on that outcome instead of the chance for ruin. Too many people spend far too much time worrying about catastrophes that never happen. This is a waste of time and energy. As a French philosopher once expressed it, "My life has been full of terrible misfortunes, most of which never happened."

TAKING RISK INVITES THE UNKNOWN

So right now ask yourself a very simple question: "How willing am I to tolerate risk?" The question is not how much risk you are willing to tolerate, but are you willing to tolerate any risk at all? Unfortunately, for many people the answer seems to be none. In his book entitled *Empires of the Mind*, author Denis Waitley makes an interesting point about the psychology of risk assessment, and about the risks of not taking risks. Waitley refers to a tribe in the Amazon region of South America who for many years had been afflicted by a rare disease. Eventually a group of physicians became friendly with the tribesmen and discovered the source of their problem. An insect that infested the walls of their dwellings caused the disease.

At that point there were three clear choices open to the members of this Amazon tribe. They could allow the doctors to spray their huts with a pesticide. They could also build new huts in a different location where the insect was not found, or they could choose to do nothing. It may seem strange to us that the last alternative is the one they chose, but as Waitley points out, for many people this should seem like a perfectly understandable response. After all, both the pesticide and moving to new homes involved a confrontation with the unknown. Both also involved a certain amount of risk. The pesticide might prove to be harmful in some way, just as there might be unforeseen problems in any new location the tribe might choose for themselves.

So they decided to stay with the predictable amount of suffering and early death they had grown used to. The risk of danger seemed worse than the danger already present. How different is this from things we see every day in our own environment? How different is this, for example, from people who stay in careers that provide little more than the illusion of security, or who live all their lives within a few blocks of where they grew up. They remain there not because they like it, but because anywhere else would be different.

USING INTUITION AS A GUIDE

That's one end of the risk tolerance spectrum. It's zero tolerance for risks. At the other end of that spectrum are people who not only tolerate risk, but who hardly even notice it at all. It may seem surprising that this category includes many very successful people, especially entrepreneurs. These individuals simply don't see their ideas as liable to failure.

Studies of wealthy entrepreneurs show that intuition is their guide. Business schools teach sophisticated mathematical approaches to risk analysis, but entrepreneurs don't use them. Those methods are for bankers and accountants. You may use these methods yourself. You can be a leader, and you can choose an acceptable level of risk. You can decide to stay away from the roller-coaster ride that many entrepreneurs have chosen. If, however, you feel uncomfortable with any level of risk whatsoever, if the status quo seems so precious that you dare not tamper with it, you must ask yourself whether you're really committed to achieving leadership mastery. After all, it's misguided to think that if you keep doing what you've always done, you'll get anything different from what you've always gotten. So you may need to decide to either lower your expectations, or raise your tolerance for risk at least a couple of notches.

ACTION STEPS

1. To get comfortable with taking risks, you need to know where you stand. On a scale from one to ten, how open are you to taking risks (one being not very open, and ten being extremely open and willing)?

   1   2   3   4   5   6   7   8   9   10

   Not open   *Extremely open*

2. To continue investigating how much risk you are willing to take, it helps to look at your experiences with risk in the past. What are some of the biggest risks you've taken in your personal and professional life? How did risk affect you, both at the time and when you look back on the situation from the perspective of months or years? Write your thoughts on three different risky situations that you have experienced.

3. Take some time to review your current life. Where might you be willing to take some risks? These risks could involve investigating a career change (if it's something you have always wanted to do), relationship opportunities, additional hobbies, travel, additional sources of income, entrepreneurial ventures, or any other area of your life in which you've considered taking action, but have perhaps feared taking risks. List at least three items that you will take action on. Be as specific as possible, and set dates to further motivate yourself and hold yourself accountable.

Tame your worries and energize your life.

—Dale Carnegie

CHAPTER 8

Confronting Risk Aversion

In this chapter we will explore ways you can assess risks, how you can turn away from poor choices, and how you can embrace those that have a real chance of paying off. We'll also look at practical techniques to make you more comfortable with risk-taking, because as a leader you should not lie awake nights worrying. You should enjoy the challenges that come with success. Finally we'll discuss how you can exercise leadership in helping others deal with risks and the setbacks that sometimes accompany it.

WORRY CAN BE PARALYZING

No one can achieve anything—certainly not leadership mastery—by consistently and exclusively focusing attention on what can go wrong. A lot of things can go wrong, but most aren't as harmful as worrying about them.

Freeman Dyson (b. 1923) is one of the most honored and accomplished physicists of his generation. Along with his work on topics such as quantum field theory and nuclear engineering, Dyson has also been fascinated by such down-to-earth topics as the physics of bicycles. He has pointed out that successful bicycle design only came by trial and error and that designing a theoretical model for bicycle operation would be a huge challenge. "It's very difficult to understand just why a bicycle works," Dyson has said. In fact, if we started to think about it too closely, we might never be able to ride around the block. But effective leaders don't get caught up in thinking about why things can't work. They know there's a risk factor in everything. They realize that there's a certain amount of faith and mystery even in mundane activities like bicycle riding. But that doesn't prevent them from getting on and pedaling away.

Risk is essential and once you've committed yourself to accepting a certain amount of risk as a step toward leadership mastery, there are ways to make it easier in your everyday life. Consider, for example, the mathematical probability of a given risk coming true, versus the fear you attach to it. Are you worried about having confrontations with your supervisor at work?

Begin keeping a written record of the number of times that anxiety actually enters your consciousness over the course of a day. This doesn't have to be anything elaborate. Just carry a piece of paper and make a check mark every time you worry about fighting with your boss. On the other side of the paper, note the number of times this confrontation has actually materialized. When you divide the number of arguments by the number of thoughts, you'll have the real probability of facing the situation. Even if you don't go through the whole mathematical process, just keeping a count of your negative thoughts can bring their number down dramatically.

FEARING RISK IS THE TRAP

Once this happens you'll see that risk itself is not usually the problem. It's the fear of risk that intrudes on our daily lives. Sometimes, of course, challenges really will materialize. Leaders accept this; they know it won't put them out of the game forever and in fact it will ultimately make them stronger. But it can be painful. It can sting, but once it's happened, you need to live with it and move on. If you accept the level of risk that every leader must learn to take on, a certain number of unpleasant realities will come into your life. Murphy's Law may not be completely accurate. After all, buttered bread doesn't always fall facedown, but Murphy was definitely onto something.

There are real problems in the real world. Most of them have remedies, but there will always be issues beyond your reach. Learn to accept them and go forward. As the old proverb says, "The dogs bark but the caravan moves on." In any case, it's not circumstances themselves that make us happy or unhappy. It's our responses to them. It's how we react to them. Since we have no choice about accepting the inevitable, struggling against it just leads to disappointment and bitterness.

As the philosopher William James wrote, acceptance of what has happened is the first step to overcoming the consequences of any misfortune. Perhaps Mother Goose put it even more eloquently when she stated, "For every ailment under the sun there is a remedy or there is none. If there be one, try to find it. If there be none, never mind it."

COMMUNICATING THE PRINCIPLES IS IMPORTANT

As a leader it's vital that you take these principles to heart and communicate them to others. This is really a three-part process. First, make it very clear that failure avoidance is not a sought-after goal. Failure is certainly not desired, but risk of failure is perfectly acceptable as long as there is a greater probability of success.

Second, if and when something does go wrong, examine what happened in a proactive framework with a focus on the future. Third, encourage team members to take risks again if the odds seem favorable.

Within those general guidelines some interesting questions

can arise. A young woman named Andrea owned a small graphic design business. Recently she'd had an opportunity for a big order from a major firm. It was a much larger job than anything she had previously undertaken, and it would require the purchase of some expensive new equipment.

This would mean taking on some large, short-term debt, since she would have to pay for the equipment now. Her fee from the new client, however, would not arrive for at least thirty days after the job was completed. Andrea spoke to her father about the situation. After a long career in business, he was now retired and acted as something of a leadership master for his daughter. Although he understood that it could be scary for Andrea to sign checks for machines she couldn't really afford at present, the real risk in the situation was more in her mind than in the material world.

True, things could go wrong. The big client could drop her in the middle of the job, her office could burn down, or she could get a severe electric shock from one of the new computers and wind up in the hospital. On the whole, though, this struck Andrea's father as a very acceptable business proposition, and one in which the risks were well worth taking. So Andrea's hand trembled as she signed the checks, but she went ahead and signed them.

This was a situation in which the leader's role was to act as a reality principle in the risk acceptance process. Andrea's father pointed out the difference between what might happen in her worst nightmare, and what was actually likely to happen. By not taking the risk, Andrea would certainly avoid all risk of failure, but she'd also back away from the reasonable risks that are a fundamental part of success.

Steve Avoids Detrimental Risk

Something like the reverse of this story involved a Los Angeles wholesale jewelry company. Steve, the owner of the company, had traveled to Italy to meet with manufacturers of gold chains and bracelets. One of the manufacturers offered Steve an incredibly good price on a large shipment of gold jewelry, provided Steve paid cash up front. Steve knew that he could make an enormous profit on the shipment, because it was so large and the price was so good.

On the other hand, the upfront payment was more than his entire bank account. He would have to take a second mortgage on his house to raise the money, but he was prepared to do that because the upside potential was so great. First, however, Steve spoke with a colleague who had an office in the same building. It's a good thing he did, because the colleague pointed out some unacceptable risks involved in the deal.

First, Steve had never done business with this supplier before. If something went wrong, it would be difficult to find any recourse. So once the money went to Italy there would be a period of time when the other party had the cash, and Steve had nothing but an assurance that the shipment would be forthcoming. Furthermore, Steve's company was already doing well. Was it wise to risk everything to get a new Mercedes? He was already driving a new Lexus. This talk with his colleague brought Steve to his senses. He backed out of the deal. Later he heard that another jeweler had gone for it, and had received a totally different shipment of goods from what he'd been led to expect. He risked good money up front and had gotten next to nothing in return.

By staying out of the gold jewelry purchase, Steve was not being too defensive. He was not engaging in failure avoidance for its own sake. Instead he was distancing himself from a situation that was tempting but had many unacceptable risks, risks to which he was temporarily blind because of his dreams of a big payoff. Steve's friend had performed an important leadership role by pointing out the enormous risks.

LEARNING FROM POOR RISK CHOICES

If and when a risk does go bad, a leader should help clarify what happened in a way that avoids punitive judgments (unless someone really acted irresponsibly). There's nothing to be gained by finger pointing, especially since leadership masters themselves always accept overall responsibility for everything that happens on their watch. In discussions like this, it's important to identify the things that went wrong as accurately as possible. It's rarely real negligence that allows risks to go bad.

Often there were good intentions that were simply impossible to fulfill. Andy, for example, graduated from an Ivy League law school and joined an elite Wall Street firm. Having paid for his entire education with scholarships and student loans, Andy was almost incredulous at the amount of money he was suddenly being paid. He was also eager to pay off his debts as quickly as possible. Moreover, he was determined to work twice as hard as any of the associate lawyers. So Andy took on too much too soon, both financially and in his workload. When he started making mistakes in some of his assignments, a conference with one of the firm's partners helped put the problem in focus.

The risk for Andy was not based on anything he was doing wrong. The risk came from trying to do too many things right. A good leader will see that this is a matter of quantity over quality. It's a time for redirection and reorientation, not for recrimination. If a leader has performed these functions effectively everyone should feel renewed enthusiasm. It may sound trite, but the best way to recover after being thrown from a horse is to get back on one. This is something leadership masters never fail to communicate to their organizations, not only in words but also in their actions.

LIFE CAN BE A DARING ADVENTURE

Right now how do you deal with risks and occasional failure on your part, by people you work with, or even by members of your family? What do you think? What do you say? Most important, what do you do toward becoming a model of risk acceptance, real-world performance, and resilience when things go wrong?

As previously mentioned, the Dancoff error principle states:

"Evolution is optimized by a maximum number of mistakes consistent with survival." Many years ago the German philosopher Friedrich Nietzsche, expressed a similar idea in rather less technical language. Nietzsche wrote, "Whatever doesn't kill me makes me stronger." But it may have been Helen Keller who best expressed the leadership master's approach to risk and indeed to life itself. "Security is mostly a superstition," Helen Keller wrote. "It does not exist in nature . . . Life is either a daring adventure or nothing."

ACTION STEPS

1. Worrying can cause emotional, physical, and mental stress in your life. How much do you worry when you have a major decision to make? Rate yourself on this scale from one to ten (one, you worry very little, and ten, you worry a great deal).

   1   2   3   4   5   6   7   8   9   10

   Worry very little   *Worry a great deal*

2. Worrying extensively can really paralyze you and keep you from making choices that could benefit your life. Write about something currently worrying you. Make a list of the worst possible outcomes and then reflect on that list. Could you handle the worst-case scenario? Most often we find that when we imagine the worst, the worry becomes less intense. Be sure to practice this exercise to move beyond worry and into action.

3. It is important to get good advice from a wise friend or mentor when you take a large risk. Make a list of at least three such mentors or friends you could contact should you need advice on major "risky" decisions.

Use encouragement.

—Dale Carnegie

CHAPTER 9

Inspirational Leadership

RESILIENT VISIONARIES

Throughout his career, Dale Carnegie was fond of relating a story about his namesake, Andrew Carnegie. Andrew was the founder of the United States Steel Corporation, and one of the wealthiest men in the history of American business. Long before he became rich, he had the gift of inspiring people to move in the direction of his leadership. They responded, not just because he told them what he wanted them to do, but also because they themselves wanted to do it.

When he was a ten-year old boy in his native Scotland, Andrew Carnegie had two pets, a father rabbit and a mother rabbit. As nature ran its course Andrew awoke one morning to find that he now had a whole nest of baby rabbits with nothing to feed them. And then he had a brilliant idea. He gathered the boys and girls in the neighborhood and offered them a special proposition. If they went out every day and picked enough grass, dandelions, and clover to feed the rabbits, Andrew would name the baby animals in their honor. The plan worked like magic and Andrew Carnegie had learned an important principle about leadership mastery and about the particular style of inspirational leadership mastery that will be the subject of this chapter.

Andrew Carnegie never forgot that incident with the rabbits, and years later he made millions of dollars using the same technique in the steel business. He wanted to sell steel rails to the Pennsylvania Railroad, whose president was J. Edgar Thomson. So, remembering the lesson from his childhood, Andrew Carnegie built a huge steel mill in Pittsburgh and named it the J. Edgar Thomson Steel Works. Soon after, when the Pennsylvania railroad needed steel rails, where do you suppose J. Edgar Thomson bought them?

It shouldn't be surprising that this instance of inspirational leadership derives from a youthful incident, because this is the kind of leadership we all want to embody at some early point in our lives: firefighter, airline pilot, doctor, or nurse. When we are kids and we aspire to these professions, what we really want to be is an inspirational leader. We want to be the one in whom people place their trust. We want to help people. We want people to give us responsibility and we want to live up to it.

LEADERS WHO INSPIRE THROUGHOUT THE AGES

In its genuine form, inspirational leadership is nothing short of a miraculous process. Truly inspirational leaders include some of the world's most admirable and remarkable people. This has been the case not just in our own time, but also throughout history.

When Hernán Cortés led Spanish soldiers in the conquest of Mexico, he did something that very clearly expresses the basic nature of inspirational leadership. Just after the soldiers had landed at what is now Veracruz, they saw that every one of their ships had just been set on fire. In other words, there was no turning back. The message that Cortés was sending to his men was very simple: Anything less than success was simply not an option. They would succeed because their leader had given them no alternative.

It's worth noting that when inspirational leaders make a statement like this, it's done in a very vivid and dramatic manner. Cortés didn't just order one of his subordinates to read a memo to the troops. He made his point in a genuinely charismatic fashion. This is very characteristic of inspirational leaders, as we'll see in this chapter and the one that follows. The content of one leader's message may be the same as another's, but the manner in which it's delivered is what defines your leadership style.

DEFINING LEADERSHIP STYLE

Johnny Bench had a tremendously successful career in major league baseball as a catcher with the Cincinnati Reds. He once defined what the role of inspirational leadership meant to him. Bench said that he wanted the pressure to be on him. He wanted his teammates to give him responsibility for winning or losing the game, because he knew he could handle it. Like Johnny, we may want this type of leadership when we're young and even strive to be that kind of leader. As we get older, though, many of us go to great lengths to avoid this type of leadership.

Many of us are right to avoid it, because not everyone is cut out to be an inspirational leader. As you read this chapter, you'll surely find much to admire in the people we'll discuss. You may also discover limits to the concept of inspirational leadership that you were not aware of.

In sum, the purpose of this chapter is not to tell you whether or not you should be an inspirational leader. Instead, it is to show you exactly what inspirational leadership is, to define its strengths and weaknesses, and to let you make your own decision about its congruency with your own style of leadership mastery.

THE INSPIRATIONAL LEADER AS THE WINNER

Let's begin by focusing on a specific quality of inspirational leadership. It is the sense that we're all in a game, that there are winners and losers, and that I, as the inspirational leader, am most definitely a winner. If you follow me, and if you perform as I encourage you to perform, you will also win. We will be part of a winning team together.

Not everybody wins all the time, however, and even the most inspirational leaders eventually encounter setbacks or defeats. In fact, because of their highly emotional nature, even the most successful inspirational leaders experience ups and downs in their careers. When a down cycle takes place, one of the most interesting characteristics of inspirational leadership comes into sharp focus. Although this kind of leader is eager to accept the pressure and responsibility for success, he or she may not be able to take responsibility for failure. The high self-esteem of inspirational leaders sometimes does not allow for the possibility that they could fall short. There must be some other explanation, and inspirational leaders are very good at finding it before they go on to their next adventure.

The Leadership of Ted Turner

The fascinating career of Ted Turner provides some very clear examples of this. In 1977, Turner won the America's Cup sailing race with a badly outdated craft named *Courageous* that seemed to be no match for the high-tech boat from Australia. Despite the team-oriented nature of sailboat racing, Turner transformed the contest into a highly personalized endeavor. He had a dream, a dream that his old secondhand boat would win the race simply on the strength of his own inspiration, and that's exactly what happened.

Turner took the triumph very personally and there was something childishly endearing about his capacity to do so. Turner simply believed he was the greatest. He couldn't help communicating that belief to the world around him, whether it was his own crew, the news media, or the competition. In the 1977 race, this force of pure belief may well have turned the tide of victory.

Three years later, however, Turner and his crew faced a very different kind of leadership in Dennis Connor. An organizational leader of the first rank, Connor prepared for the 1980 race with more hours on the water than the combined total of all the other challengers. Turner badly underestimated Connor, and the race selection committee excused Turner's boat during the preliminary trials. It was a crushing and even humiliating defeat for someone who had been so eager to personalize the competition, but he very clearly was not fazed. In contrast to how they regard victories, inspirational leaders let defeats pass right through them with little visible effect. Ted Turner never sailed again in competition. He even sold the boat in which he had won the legendary 1977 race, but his sense of himself as a born winner was absolutely intact. He just set off in pursuit of another dream.

CREATE, COMMUNICATE, AND PURSUE DREAMS

The ability to create, communicate, and pursue dreams is, in fact, the first defining quality of inspirational leadership. Inspirational leadership masters see a clear picture of the future in their mind's eye. The dream has tangible reality. It's like Mount Everest: It's there and the leader is going to lead his team to the top. Masters of inspirational leadership not only make their dreams seem real, they can enlist others in the pursuit of those same dreams simply through the energy of their own charismatic personalities.

To put it another way, inspirational leaders have the ability to transfer importance. They have an almost magical power to take what is important to them and make it important to other people. Conversely, they have a decided lack of interest in what someone else might consider a priority. They simply don't worry about what's on other people's minds, and before long others aren't worrying either. This is what transferring importance really means.

The pilot of a paramedic helicopter expressed this very well in an interview for a book entitled *Bosses*, written by Jim Wall.

"You've got to learn to lead people to the decision you want," the pilot said, "but they need to feel that it was their idea. This is not just telling someone what to do; it's telling them what you want and intend to do, and having them want and intend the same thing. It's also inspiring the belief that the goal is really possible, that it really can be obtained with the help of inspired leadership."

From very early on in the history of Microsoft, Bill Gates had a vision. It was something that he saw very clearly, and something that he communicated with great verve. It was a vision that he saw as much more important than anything anyone else might suggest. The vision was this: a personal computer on every desk in America. It's clear, it's simple, and at least when Gates presents it, the image of two hundred million personal computers on two hundred million desks can even sound inspirational.

Similarly, when Steven Jobs and Steve Wozniak were in that now-famous garage creating Apple Computer Inc., they both had visions but not exactly the same ones. Wozniak was the more technically oriented of the two. He thought in terms of operating systems, processors, and hard-disk memory. The vision Jobs had was much more down to earth. He imagined a computer that came in a box. It was as simple as that: a machine that you could buy in a box, just like a radio or a microwave oven. It was a machine that you could take home and plug in, and it would work.

Why was this such a compelling vision? Once again it was simple, easily communicated, and at a time when computer components were bought one piece at a time, it was quite revolutionary. At the very moment when Jobs came up with his vision of a computer in a box, people with Scotch tape on their glasses and plastic penholders in their shirt pockets comprised the majority of computing enthusiasts. Basically they were people like Steve Wozniak. Having known people like that close-up, Steve Jobs knew there would never be enough of them to create the revolution he dreamed of.

He knew he had to reach the millions of people who formed

mainstream society, the people who were used to buying things that came in boxes. So Jobs took the very complex and problematic task of introducing personal computing to America, and reduced it to a very simple and literal idea. The computer had to come in a box.

Steve Jobs was a master of inspirational leadership. He was able to communicate his vision and convince others to commit themselves to it just as deeply as he himself had. The ability to express a dream through a simple, tangible, down-to-earth image is essential to this kind of leader. Think about this the next time you are called upon to discuss a project or motivate a development team.

Managing Versus Genuine Leadership

Robert J. Eaton was a chairman and CEO of the former Daimler-Chrysler Corporation. It was the world's third largest car-maker in terms of total revenue. The company was formed in 1998 by the merger of Chrysler and Daimler-Benz. In its first year after the merger, net income was more than six billion dollars. Although Eaton had a technical background with a degree in mechanical engineering, he valued inspirational leadership very highly.

Eaton believed that the requirements for running a big company had changed dramatically in the twenty years prior to his leadership. In describing those changes, he made a sharp distinction between what he called managing and genuine leadership. "A manager is someone who thinks in primarily quantitative terms, numbers, units, quarters, fiscal years. A leader thinks in terms of people and ideas." At DaimlerChrysler, Bob Eaton believed that he should devote less time to managing, and more time to leading. For one thing, the pure numbers of business change so fast that focusing on them almost becomes an exercise in futility, especially for a CEO. The time simply isn't available for running all the numbers and keeping track of the results. Instead a leader needs to create vision and beliefs and values. A leader needs to break through creative roadblocks and inspire people to fulfill their potential (even if they have not yet discovered their true potential).

In an interview, Bob Eaton put it this way: "A leader is someone who can take a group of people to a place they themselves don't think they can go." This, in fact, is a perfect definition of inspirational leadership.

INSPIRE YOURSELF TO INSPIRE YOUR TEAM

Whether you're already a senior manager or still an aspiring leader, you'll need to know how to encourage teamwork in your organization. This is an essential business skill. Building a team involves more than just putting the right people together.

If you have the power to handpick your team, make an assessment of their strengths and weaknesses to ensure the best combination of skills. Surround yourself with good people, but not people who are all good at the same thing. Be careful not to choose clones, especially clones of yourself. Diversity is always good as long as individuals are willing and able to work together.

Sometime you may be assigned to lead a group of people who have no interest in being part of a team. This is a chance to really test your leadership abilities. How can you create an environment in which each individual wants to work cooperatively and collaboratively? This is where the ability to inspire and implement teamwork becomes essential. Here are a few more guiding principles to point you in the right direction.

See the Big Picture

Make sure everyone grasps the long-range goals of the company. Reinforce those goals as often as possible. People may become so focused on today's problems and routine duties that they lose sight of the big picture. When some members of the team concentrate on putting out fires, others can dedicate more time to reviewing longer-range strategies to forestall future problems.

Clarify Roles

Outline the duties and responsibilities of everyone on the team. Understanding one another's duties and deadlines always helps people work collaboratively. Encourage the team members to define the division tasks among themselves. They'll take on more responsibility if they are in control, and someone may even emerge as a previously untapped talent.

Set Goals

Team members need to develop individual and group objectives. As a leader, you can urge them to set achievable and measurable short-term aspirations as well as long-term ones. With collective, team-driven goals and a shared code of ethics, the group will begin to self-direct. Peer pressure and individual pride will help foster responsibility and peak performance.

Share Information

Share as much information as you can to prevent gossip and rumor-mongering. A rumor mill is a drain on productivity and morale. Earn your team's respect and confidence with openness and honesty. During periods of change or crises, reveal as much as you can as soon as possible and promise to update team members as soon as you can.

Build Trust

This is very simple. Keep your word. Be trustworthy and dependable. If you're a sales manager and you promise a day off with pay if the sales team meets its target, follow through on that promise. If you're a team member and offer to obtain information for a colleague, make that information a priority. Treat all members of the team consistently and fairly and don't play favorites.

Pay Attention

Be open to the team's ideas, whether they're presented as a formal written submission or in a brainstorming session. Consider every suggestion and respond to the individual or entire team, whichever is more appropriate. Many organizations spend hundreds of thousands of dollars on consultants without first asking employees for their ideas on productivity, new products, or cost cutting.

Be Patient

If the team does not seem to come together at first, give team members some time to get along. Watch patiently but closely to see if they can resolve their differences on their own. If not, you may have to reassign one or more individuals. Otherwise the success of the team may be compromised.

Offer Encouragement

Challenge each team member to participate and contribute, but do this in a positive, results-oriented way. Urge them to take additional training, if need be, and to step beyond their comfort zones to develop their unique talents. Shift people's responsibilities regularly and often. Acknowledge each individual's strengths and offer positive reinforcement and encouragement.

Praise the Team Generously

Celebrate the team's achievements together. Reward the team as a whole, not individual members. Sometimes a person will excel at everything. Recognize this privately and through the performance review process. But for the sake of continued teamwork, eliminate any opportunity for jealousy and resentment. Always speak positively about your team. Display their talents and publicly recognize their dedication, their efforts, and their successes.

Be Enthusiastic

Enthusiastic energy is contagious. Be positive, upbeat, and hopeful. Expect great things from your team and they'll do their best not to disappoint you. A real leader knows how to focus on what's going right even when everything seems to be going wrong.

Make It Fun

Team spirit is energizing and unifying, so make time to enjoy being with the group. Join them for lunch occasionally or for a beer after work. Picnics and outings to sports or entertainment events can also be excellent morale builders. When team members see each other as unique human beings, cooperation and willingness to work hard will naturally increase.

Ease Up

Theodore Roosevelt said, "The best executive is one who has sense enough to pick good people . . . and self-restraint enough to keep from meddling with them." So keep the number of rules as low as possible. "Because we've always done it that way" is not an acceptable reason for anything. To the greatest extent possible, let the team itself determine how to work together. For instance, unless you're operating an assembly line, flexible starting times may increase productivity. Flexibility with all preexisting rules is an important key to successful teamwork.

Delegate, Delegate, Delegate

Explain what needs to be done, explain how to do it—and then let go. Better yet, describe the problem and the desired result and let the team develop an action plan together. Trust the individuals and the collective team to complete their assigned tasks successfully and on time. If you've set a project review meeting for next

Tuesday, resist the temptation to ask for an update today. Have confidence that the team will meet the deadline.

Above All, Inspire!

When you're in charge of a team, lead by example. Say "we" more often than "I"—but always understand that the buck stops with you. If something goes wrong, take responsibility without blaming others. When the right time comes, discuss the problems calmly with the team.

ACTION STEPS

1. Andrew Carnegie showed signs of inspirational leadership during his youth. Reflect on your childhood. What leadership initiative did you display at an early age? Write about any creative, inspirational, or bold initiatives you took when you were growing up.

2. From the following list, select the five individuals you personally find the most inspirational. After each name that you select, briefly describe the specific traits that you admire.

Muhammad Ali	Bill Gates	Elvis Presley
Warren Buffet	Jim Henson	Christopher Reeve
Bill Clinton	Michael Jordan	Eleanor Roosevelt
Hillary Clinton	John F. Kennedy	Steven Spielberg
Walter Cronkite	Martin Luther King, Jr.	Barbara Walters
Walt Disney	Rosa Parks	Tiger Woods

3. Go through the traits that you listed in #2, and mark those that you currently possess with a ✓, and mark those that you do not with an X. Make a commitment and devise an action plan to cultivate those traits you marked with an X.

Leaders never lose their focus. They keep their eyes on the big picture.

—Dale Carnegie

CHAPTER 10

A Profile of the Inspirational Leader

By now it should be clear that an inspirational leader is a kind of poet. Inspirational leaders don't usually like routine. They want to keep opening up new territories. They can be impatient with details and are often not very good at small talk. They tend to see themselves as the lead roles in a great drama that they're enacting with the other members of the organization. If they give themselves the best lines, it's only because they genuinely believe those lines will bring out the best in everyone.

Clearly this style of leadership blends well with historic conquest and with America's Cup sailboat racing. It also fits with building Andrew Carnegie's steel mills and running multibillion-dollar companies.

For those of us not engaged in enterprises on that scale, inspirational leadership presents a special challenge. You may be in the children's furniture business, or you may run a pet store in a suburban shopping mall. Whatever your endeavors, you must be able to see yourself on a grand scale if you aspire to be an inspirational leader.

The single biggest challenge of inspirational leadership

mastery is the ability to play the hero. If you want to inspire, you want to have the ball in your mitt at the last second of the game. You believe that you are a rock star, even if you're on a telephone instead of a stage. Hold on to that vision.

Harvey Mackay's book *Swim with the Sharks Without Being Eaten Alive* has sold well over two million copies worldwide. From the title you might expect the book to be a memoir about an underwater demolition team or the recovery of sunken treasure. Instead it's lessons learned by running an envelope business in Minneapolis, Minnesota. It's not about locating Spanish galleons. It's about retaining customers when a competitor undercuts your unit price. Mackay's genius lies in making the envelope business sound like the Normandy invasion. He is able to do this on the printed page because he does it in his everyday life as well. He can communicate it to others because he truly believes it himself.

INSPIRATIONAL LEADERS ARE LARGER THAN LIFE

The core of inspirational leadership is the sense that things are happening on a scale larger than life. You have the ability to see your experiences in this way. What is really exciting about your work, your organization, and the people who comprise it? What are some of the really dramatic things that have taken place under your leadership? Who were the heroes of those stories, and who were the villains? When you begin to think of your world in this way, you're beginning to think like an inspirational leader.

Paul Messner owns a small graphic design company in Sacramento, California. Most of his business is with local companies who run display ads in newspapers and magazines. For its size, Paul's company is very successful. However, he has never worked on a national ad campaign, nor has his work ever run in a nationally distributed publication. Nonetheless, Paul has mastered the art of inspirational leadership. Regardless of the number of employees he has or his gross income at the end of the year, Paul's business is big because he sees it as big.

Whenever Paul hires someone, he takes half an hour with the new employee for a private conversation. The meeting is always pretty much the same, but it has such meaning for Paul that the experience seems entirely new. This is because Paul tells a story that defines what his company intends to be. On the surface it's not particularly earthshaking. There was a convention taking place in San Diego. Paul's firm had designed some brochures and booklets that would be made available at the door and during the scheduled presentations. The work had gone smoothly and everything had gone to the printer well before the convention was scheduled to begin on a Saturday morning.

It was quite a shock, therefore, when a phone call came on Friday afternoon from the convention organizers. Where were all the brochures and booklets? Paul quickly ascertained that the printer had completed the job on schedule, but had mistakenly shipped it by regular surface mail and not by express. There was no way the material would get to San Diego by the time the doors opened in the morning. All the advertising and the printed material would go to waste. If anything in this line of work could be called a genuine catastrophe, this was it.

Strictly speaking, the fault lay with the printer, but Paul felt personally responsible for it. It was now after closing time on a Friday evening, but Paul insisted that the printer stay open. He demanded that the entire job be reprinted immediately. Despite the fact that it had taken more than a week to print the job in the first place, Paul kept things moving throughout the night. Moreover, when the materials were ready, Paul put everything in the back of his truck and hit the road for San Diego. Dawn was just breaking by the time he arrived.

After hearing Paul tell this story, despite the fact that he's told it dozens of times, every new employee feels as if they are joining a company that can alter the course of world history. That's the way an inspirational leader can make people feel. It's not a matter of technique; it's passion, commitment, and high drama. It's taking something like graphic design and turning it into something like emergency heart surgery.

The hope is that even in reading this you're beginning to feel some of the excitement that comes with being an inspirational leader.

THE PRESSURES OF INSPIRATIONAL LEADERSHIP

In addition to everything inspirational leaders must give to other people, they must also be prepared to take on even more. Psychologically speaking, inspirational leaders can become like surrogate parents to their team members. And as every parent knows, this means being the focal point for all kinds of hopes, dreams, fears, and irrational hostilities. An inspirational leader can never hold this dynamic against people or punish them for their emotional investment. Nothing must be done to discourage them from making this investment, because this kind of obligation is the foundation of a leader's effectiveness. Under this kind of pressure and scrutiny, it's really no surprise that many inspirational leaders eventually leave that role.

Throughout history inspirational leadership has often been understood as a highly perishable and transitory quality. When military or political crises occurred in ancient Rome, a highly charismatic individual would be given almost dictatorial powers. They would be given this power, however, only for the duration of the problem. Similarly, American Indian tribes of the Great Plains appointed special leaders to deal with particular situations. They seemed to recognize that inspirational leaders could be expected to burn brightly, but not for long. It's important to be aware of the many pressures that this kind of mastery demands. Be sure you're ready to accept them and to live up to them.

DELEGATION AS INSPIRATION

Leaders have many ways to communicate ideas to team members. The possibilities range from simply telling people what to do to much more collaborative approaches. A number of these possibilities are described by the Tannenbaum-Schmidt Continuum, named after two researchers who worked in the '70s.

When looking over the Tannenbaum-Schmidt principles, it's important to remember a key fact: Regardless of how much responsibility and latitude a leader may delegate to a team, the leader must remain accountable for any major problems that result. Delegating freedom and decision making does not relieve the leader of accountability. For this reason, the process of delegation requires a very mature leader free from ego-based needs. If everything goes well, the team must get the credit. But if it all goes wrong, the leader has to take the blame.

Here are the Tannenbaum-Schmidt levels of delegated freedom and decision making:

LEVEL ONE: *The leader alone makes decisions and announces the course of action that will be followed.*

Here, after reviewing options in light of priorities, resources, and time frame, the leader decides what to do and simply informs the team of the decision. While the leader may have factored the team's reaction into the decision-making process, the team has no active role in actually making the decision. In fact, the team may know and accept the fact that the team's welfare is a relatively minor consideration in deciding the overall outcome. This may be the case, for instance, in military organizations, particularly in combat situations.

LEVEL TWO: *The leader decides and then sells the decision to the team.*

As in level one, the leader alone makes the decision—but now an explanation is added. The leader shares reasons for the direction to be taken, focusing on the benefits to the organization and its clients, and for the team members themselves, As a result, team members see the leader as someone who recognizes their importance and is concerned about their well-being.

LEVEL THREE: *The leader accompanies the decision with background information for the team, and also invites questions.*

Here the team is invited to ask questions and discuss with the manager the rationale behind the decision. This enables the team to understand and accept or agree with the decision more easily than in levels one and two. The hope is for the team to appreciate the issues and reasons for the decision, and the implications of all the various options. The result should be a higher level of motivation because of greater involvement and discussion by the team.

LEVEL FOUR: *The leader makes a provisional decision and invites discussion about it.*

The leader discusses and reviews the provisional decision with the team. It is understood that the leader will consider the team's views before a final decision is made. This enables the team to have some degree of real influence over the shape of the final outcome. Level four acknowledges the principle that the team can make valuable contributions to the decision-making process.

LEVEL FIVE: *The leader presents the situation or problem before making even a provisional decision.*

Here the team is encouraged and expected to offer ideas and options right from the beginning, and to discuss the implications of each possible course of action. The leader then decides which option to take. This level is most appropriate when the team has more detailed knowledge or experience of the issues than the leader.

LEVEL SIX: *The leader explains the situation, defines the boundaries, and asks the team to decide.*

At this level the leader has effectively delegated responsibility for the decision to the team, although within certain clearly stated limits. The leader may or may not choose to be a part of the team that makes the decision. While this level appears to gives a huge responsibility to the team, the leader still controls the risk and outcomes to some extent. This level requires a mature team with a deep commitment to the leader and the success of the organization as a whole.

LEVEL SEVEN: *The leader allows the team to identify issues, generate possible options, and decide on actions.*

This is the highest level of freedom for the team. The team is first given responsibility for identifying and analyzing the situation or problem. Then the team explores options and implements a course of action. The leader also states in advance that he or she will support the team's decision and will help to bring it about. If the leader takes part in discussions with the team, he or she has no more authority than anyone else during the discussion process.

Here the team must be mature and competent, and capable of thinking and acting at a strategic level.

INSPIRATION THROUGH QUESTIONING

Ian McDonald of Johannesburg, South Africa, was the general manager of a small manufacturing plant specializing in precision machine parts. When he had the opportunity to accept a very large order, he was convinced that he would not meet the promised delivery date. Work was already scheduled in the shop, and the short completion time needed for this order made it seem impossible for him to accept the order.

Instead of pushing his people to accelerate their work and rush the order through, he called everybody together. He explained the situation and told them how much it would mean to the company, and to them personally, if they could produce the order on time.

Then he started asking questions. Is there anything we can do to handle this order? Can anyone think of a different way to process it through the shop that will make it possible to take the order? Is there any way to adjust our hours or personnel assignments that would help? The employees came up with many ideas and insisted that he take the order. They approached it with a "we can do it" attitude, and the order was accepted, produced, and delivered on time.

Asking questions stimulates the creativity of the persons whom you ask. People are more likely to accept an order if they have had a part in the decision and in devising a solution.

Ian McDonald inspired his staff to find solutions to an apparently impossible situation. He had an uncanny ability to draw magical solutions from his employees. Earlier we saw how Ted Turner coped with sudden changes in his leadership fortunes. When the magic deserted him in a particular undertaking, Turner simply unplugged and moved onto something new. While this may have left people feeling abandoned, for a leader like Turner it's probably necessary to his survival. In any case, it may not be completely his choice. By its very nature, the life of an inspirational leader is like a roller-coaster ride. So are the lives of the people they lead.

In the next chapter we'll look at a very different kind of leader, and one that may be much more common at the dawn of the twenty-first century. When Louis V. Gerstner, Jr., for example, took leadership of IBM, the company was in a prolonged downward slide. There was talk of breaking up IBM. It was simply too big and unwieldy. Amid the talk of a breakup, Gerstner was asked to describe his vision of the company. His reply would make an inspirational leader cringe. "I don't have a vision," Gerstner said. "The last thing IBM needs right now is a vision." Instead of inspiring the troops with high-minded rhetoric, one of Gerstner's first acts was to ban the use of projectors in staff meetings. This proved to be an effective move, but it was hardly inspirational. Instead, it was organizational. Organizational leadership mastery is the topic of our next chapter.

ACTION STEPS

1. Based on the examples provided, make a list of both the positive and negative aspects of inspirational leadership.

2. Make a list of the individuals in your life whom you feel you can inspire. Then create an action plan to do so.

3. Take at least five minutes each day for the next week and visualize yourself as an inspirational leader. See yourself in that role, including as much detail as possible. Write about any ideas or insights you gain while doing this exercise.

Call attention to people's mistakes indirectly.

—Dale Carnegie

CHAPTER 11

Organizational Leadership

ORGANIZATIONAL LEADERS LOOK INWARD

In the previous chapter we wrote about inspirational leaders, who in many ways resemble rock stars. They are most at home at center stage, exciting the crowd to new heights of passion and devotion. Inspirational leaders can achieve huge popularity and success. They can reach the heights, and they can also fall very fast and hard. All in all, it's a risk they're glad to take. In this chapter our topic is a very different kind of leadership mastery. If inspirational leaders are like rock stars, the organizational leaders we will look at now are like music company executives or theatrical agents. Organizational leaders don't crave adulation or applause. They're often uncomfortable in the spotlight. They are not eager to accept the scrutiny and second-guessing that comes with spectacular success or failure. For their reward, organizational leaders look inward at the solid foundation they've created. They let others lead the parade through the outside world.

Lou Gerstner of IBM, for example, is a superb executive and corporate turnaround specialist. When he became head of IBM (at a time when plans were already in place to break up the once-proud company), Gerstner did something that would have been taboo to many business leaders of the past. He did nothing, at least not immediately.

Although Gerstner has described himself as intense, competitive, focused, blunt, and tough, he might have added restrained and realistic. At an early press conference he refused to present his vision for the future of the company. In fact, he said he didn't have one. Instead he quite predictably undertook some downsizing with the company, and began to reorient it toward customer service. He banned the use of projectors during meetings. While this fostered better communication, it could hardly be interpreted as a battle cry. Gerstner did, however, eventually create viable, long-term goals for IBM, and his success speaks for itself.

THE FALL OF THE CORPORATE PYRAMID

This is the way of the organizational leader, someone whose time has definitely come. In the past, whether fifty years ago or five hundred, large organizations were shaped like the pyramids of early civilization. There were large numbers of people on the bottom followed by layer after layer of supervisors and managers in ascending order. Each new layer had more authority than the one below.

This many-tiered structure rose even higher until it reached its pinnacle. That's where the king, the general, the CEO, the chairman, and the board of directors got to sit, and that's where the classic inspirational leader was also most comfortable. Was this the best way to structure an organization? Perhaps it was in many cases and at many times, especially when the leader was well suited for it. Until quite recently, however, no one really bothered to ask whether it was best. The pyramid-shaped organization was just the way things were.

In the twenty-first century, many of those pyramids have come tumbling down. Borders, ranks, and lines of demarcation are steadily evaporating. Every day new technologies are equalizing access to information and making rigid bureaucracies obsolete. You don't have to have a deep voice and big biceps to be a leader anymore. You have to be fast, flexible, and first with a new idea.

Organization leaders are very comfortable with these changes. Their authority doesn't depend on force or personality. Their first priority is the strength and success of the organization. Its size and shape are much less important. That's why organizational leaders are comfortable and sometimes even ruthless about downsizing. In fact, extreme versions of the organizational leader would just as soon employ three people as three thousand if the bottom line could be improved. This could be a serious mistake, as we'll discuss later in this chapter. However, even the most moderate organizational leader puts profitability first. If it means less glory for the leaders themselves, they see this as progress also. Rigid chains of command stifle creativity and the development of new products or services. Over time this can weaken any organization. Organizational leaders would take this development very seriously. They want their company, school, or football team to function as smoothly and as efficiently as possible. This is because it's in their nature to create streamlined organizations.

COOPERATION IS KEY

If this is your leadership style, you welcome changes that eliminate the old rigidity. You want people to be free to do their best. You regret the many years in which their talents were forced to lie dormant. Renowned management author Peter Drucker perfectly expressed the organizational leader's point of view when he said, "The modern organization cannot be an organization of boss and subordinate. It must be organized as a team." The CEO of a large multinational company put it even more concisely when he declared, "The lone ranger is just no longer possible."

As an organizational leader, you want to eliminate not only

departmental rivalries, but also the departments themselves, if it will nurture success. By the same token, you want to get rid of automatic promotions, seniority-based pay scales, and other frustrating vestiges of the old days. In old pyramid companies, engineers spent all day cooped up with other engineers. Bookkeepers sat next to other bookkeepers. Middle managers rarely interacted with either the CEO or the shipping clerk.

An organizational leader, however, doesn't hesitate to bring an engineer to a group of salespeople, throwing down a challenge to make the product more attractive to the customer, or to figure out how to build it faster. Or he may ask them to use their technical expertise to get around a marketing glitch.

In eclectic groups such as these, it's almost impossible to determine who is where on the corporate hierarchy. As Peter Drucker pointed out, the world is no longer made up of privates, officers, and drill sergeants. Modern organizational leaders thoroughly understand that. Armies were traditionally organized along a paradigm of command and control, and organizations in other fields simply copied that model.

BUILDING HORIZONTAL TEAMS

Today, with organizational leadership leading the way, groups are structured more like soccer or tennis teams than like infantry divisions. Every team member is now empowered to act as a decision maker. Employees must see themselves as both executives and line workers. Organizational leadership masters are very comfortable with that. They don't care about emptying their own wastebaskets and getting in the trenches as long as the strength of the team is enhanced.

These flattened organizations are turning up in every field from steel companies to educational institutions. As the principal of an East Coast elementary school pointed out, "There's now a real incentive to build teams and lead people from a horizontal rather than a vertical perspective." There's much less emphasis on titles, hourly pay, or other incentives. The team's performance and the strength of the organization are their own reward. This kind of effective teamwork doesn't happen overnight, and the leader needs unique skills to bring it into being.

It's a different kind of leadership than the old-fashioned pep talk in the locker room. That kind of inspirational leadership can still work in the hands of a uniquely gifted person, but fewer and fewer people are aspiring to it, and wisely so. Bill Gates in his cardigan and Steve Case in his khaki pants are the role models now. Very few of the new organizational leadership masters are comfortable in a helmet or a pair of shoulder pads.

THE ESSENTIAL INGREDIENTS OF ORGANIZATIONAL LEADERSHIP

Any organization, first and foremost, is a group of people with a shared sense of purpose. Nurturing that sense is the primary task of an organizational leader. People working together can accomplish extraordinary things. They can accomplish almost anything when they work together as part of a well-designed organization. The essence of such an organization is the unified vision of the team members. Once that vision is in place, the ideas, creativity, and innovation will come from the team itself. The leader, however, still plays an absolutely essential role.

He or she must direct and focus all that energy. Leaders must keep the team members informed about how their work affects the organization, its customers or clients, and the outside world as a whole. The president of a midsize electronics firm described what this means. "You've got to create the emotional and intellectual environment. You've got to zero in on the corporate objective. You've got to provide the stimulus and encouragement so that individuals and teams can truly think of themselves as world-class."

STRESSING GROUP PERFORMANCE
OVER INDIVIDUAL

Recognition, feedback, and shared purpose make that possible. These three elements are what the leader needs to provide. While creating a shared sense of purpose is a key element of organizational leadership, there is another way to make the same point. Leaders must make it clear that success is a group experience, as is anything short of success. Unless the whole team wins, no one wins. Individual records are fine in history books or almanacs, but they're seriously out of place in today's most competitive organizations.

Organizational leaders believe that what matters most—in fact, the only thing that matters at all—is the performance of the whole group. Once you get people committed to this, it is contagious. "They reinforce one another," says one CEO. It's more like playing for the World Cup than working on an assembly line. There's a whole different energy level, a new kind of collective intensity.

People need to feel important. If they're denied that feeling, they'll give less than full effort to the project at hand. So an effective organizational leader lets as many decisions as possible pass through the entire group. As an organizational leader, let the ideas bubble up in all the members of the team. Don't dictate solutions. Don't insist that things be done a certain way.

A small manufacturing company in Cleveland provides a good illustration of this. The company had a problem. A very large order was being negotiated, but the buyer insisted on a seemingly impossible delivery date. The company president could have imposed a solution from the top down, but instead he asked a team of his employees to come up with a plan. Their response was, "If we shuffle some other things around, we feel we can make the delivery date," and that's what happened. If the president had made the decision himself, he would probably have backed away from the order. Either that or he might have angered his workers by pushing them too hard. When they made the choice them-selves, however, there was a collective decision being made. With a group effort at the helm of this ship, they were steered back on course, and the outcome was totally positive.

RECOGNIZING THE COLLECTIVE CONTRIBUTION

Maybe that's why masters of organizational leadership use words like *we* and *us* a lot more than *I* and *me*. Leadership masters always emphasize how everyone's contribution fits in. If the ad man does great work, but the packaging specialist fails, that's not success. If the marketing director hits a home run, but the production people strike out, the whole team loses. When everybody contributes to the best of their ability, from the person who answers the phones to the person who signs the checks, that's a win for all of them.

If leaders do their jobs correctly, there's an almost paradoxical quality to this kind of collective effort, because the individuality of the team members somehow remains intact. They still have different skills. They still have unique personalities. They still have different hopes and fears. Talented organizational leaders recognize those differences, appreciate them, and use them for the benefit of the group. Leaders believe firmly in every member of the team and are eager to express that belief whenever possible.

When mistakes occur, good organizational leaders avoid point-ing the finger of blame at any one individual. If there's a problem, they speak privately with team members about how results can be improved. They do not single people out, nor do they talk about the weak link in the chain. Whether it's a high school classroom, a manufacturing plant, or a corporate boardroom, the organiza-tional leader's purpose is to optimize performance by building spirit within the group. The team is encouraged to set its own standards, and members look forward to living up to them. They feel great about themselves when they make the grade, and their efforts become even more focused.

THE LEADER AS A CONSTANT PRESENCE

And all this, of course, eventually expresses itself in the numbers on the balance sheet. To make this happen, the leader has to be a constant presence. In old-fashioned pyramid-style companies it was easy for the boss to remain relatively aloof. This has all changed in today's most effective organizations. Leaders have to be there physically, and they must be intellectually and emotionally tuned in.

The president of a major hospital on Long Island says learning how to listen can take a while, but if you work hard at it, you develop a great feel for everything that is going on around you. It's like standing on the deck of an aircraft carrier with all those planes landing and taking off. Every one of those planes has to be very important to you, and at the same time the ship has to stay on course and be protected from attack. You eventually learn to factor all those considerations together.

Organizational leaders are aware of at least two objectives that must constantly be serviced with every team member. The first goal is successful performance of the job at hand. The second goal is that every job should also be a training experience leading to even better performance and greater responsibility in the future. In other words, leaders must strengthen the organization by developing new business and getting jobs done on time. They must strengthen it by honing the skills of all the organization's members. The political columnist Walter Lippmann expressed this principle very eloquently: "The final test of leaders that they leave behind them in others the conviction and the will to carry on." In short, organizational leaders should take genuine responsibility for the development and careers of the entire team.

ASKING THE RIGHT QUESTIONS

"How would you like to improve?" the leader should frequently ask. "Where do you want your career to go from here? What kinds of new responsibilities would you like to be taking on?" It is the leader's job to ask those questions, and to respond in ways that help team members achieve their goals. In other words, you need to communicate the confidence you have in their abilities. You should provide standards for the organization to meet or exceed, and publicly show your appreciation when that happens. Remember, for an effective organizational leader, team success equals personal success. Anything else is unacceptable. The greatest reward these leaders can achieve is to inspire, mentor, and model into being a group of talented, confident, motivated, and cooperating people who are themselves ready to lead.

MEETINGS: CAN'T LIVE WITH THEM, CAN'T LIVE WITHOUT THEM

Meetings are actually a very expensive business activity, once the cost per participant is factored in. As a result, meetings really need to be well run and well led. Poorly run meetings waste time, money, and resources—and are far worse than no meetings at all.

The need for effective, organized meetings has become even more intense with the increasing demands on people's time, and the fact that members of an organization may not be in the same workplace or even in the same country. Fortunately, new technologies provide alternatives to conventional face-to-face meetings around a table. Phone and videoconferencing, for example, can save time and money. Still, there will always be a trade-off between the efficiencies of virtual meetings and the limitations of remote communications methods, especially when the video or audio connection is lost just as the meeting leader was about to make an important point.

Effective leaders choose meeting methods that are appropriate for the situation. Is a physical presence really necessary? Leaders should explore options such as phone and videoconferencing before deciding that a physical meeting is required.

A face-to-face meeting is the best option for conveying feelings and meanings. For very serious matters, this should always be the first choice. Meanings and feelings can be lost or confused when people are not physically sitting in the same room as each other. Trying to save time and money by holding virtual meetings for really important issues is often self-defeating. It may also be unfair to team members if the issue significantly affects their futures or well-being.

Basically, a well-led meeting is a unique opportunity in two ways. It's a chance to achieve an outcome that benefits the organization as a whole, and also to benefit individual team members in a variety of ways. Leaders should approach all meetings with these two different but mutually supporting aims in mind.

Regardless of the topic, at the close of a successful meeting both the leader and the team members should feel that their unique needs were met, and that the items on the agenda were covered.

Meeting Components

As a leader, your choices of the structure and style of an effective meeting depends on a number of factors, including:

- The specific situation, including background, future concerns, and urgency

- The organizational context, including implications and needs for you, your team, and the organization

- The needs and interests of the attendees

- Your own needs and interests, as well as your authority, confidence, and other leadership qualities

Actually, meetings will always have more than one objective. Aside from the specific concerns that have brought the participants together, there are also their personal, individual agendas (and yours), as well as the need to further develop the team as a highly functioning professional entity.

Whenever you call and conduct a meeting, you are making demands on people's time and attention. As a leader you have authority to do this, but you need to use it wisely. Whatever the explicit reason for the meeting, you have a responsibility to bring it into being as a positive and helpful experience for all who attend.

Having this overall aim, alongside the specific meeting objectives, will help you develop an ability and reputation as an effective, results-oriented leader.

Basic Guidelines

Meetings that encourage participation and shared responsibility will obviously be more constructive than those in which the leader simply lectures and hands down decisions. Below are some basic guidelines that can be applied to many different sorts of meetings. They assume you have considered properly and concluded that the meeting is necessary, and also that you have decided what sort of meeting to hold.

1. Plan carefully, using an agenda format as a planning tool.

2. Circulate the meeting agenda in advance.

3. Run the meeting effectively. Keep control. Agree on outcomes and responsibilities. Take notes.

4. Write and circulate the notes, emphasizing actions and responsibilities.

5. Follow up with team members based on the notes that were circulated.

Meeting Priorities

Here's a good rule of thumb. Always have a clear purpose for a meeting. Otherwise, don't have a meeting in the first place. Decide the issues for the meeting and their relative importance and urgency. The issues may be very different and may need to be treated in different ways. Something may be important, for example, without the need for urgent resolution. Issues that are both urgent and important are clearly serious priorities that need careful planning and immediate action.

Meeting Outcomes

Decide the type of outcome envisioned for each issue and put this on the agenda alongside the item heading. This is important, because team members need to know what is expected of them. Also, meetings will be more productive when the aims are clear at the outset. For each issue, typical outcomes include:

- Decision

- More discussion needed

- More information needed

- Planning sessions needed

- Feedback needed

- Team-building to begin

Meeting Sequence

Put the less important issues at the top of the agenda, not at the end. If you put them at the end, you may never get to them because all your time has been spent on the big issues.

Be aware that people are most sensitive at the beginning of meetings, especially if there are attendees who are eager to make their presence felt. It can be helpful to schedule controversial issues later in the agenda, which gives people a chance to settle down and relax.

Timing

Leaders should consider the time required for various agenda items rather than habitually or arbitrarily decide the length of the meeting. Give each item a realistic time frame. Keep the timings realistic, and remember that things usually take longer than you think.

Plan plenty of breaks for long meetings. Unless people are participating and fully involved, their concentration begins to drop after just forty-five minutes. Breaks need to be twenty minutes for coffee and pastries. Ten minutes every hour for a breath of fresh air and a leg-stretch will help keep people attentive.

Unless you have a specific reason for arranging one, avoid a formal sit-down lunch break. That just makes people drowsy. Working lunches are great, but make sure you give people ten to fifteen minutes to get some fresh air and move around outside the meeting room. If the venue can only provide lunch in a restaurant, arrange a buffet. If a sit-down meal is unavoidable, save time by giving the menu choices to the restaurant earlier in the day.

It's helpful to put planned times for each item on the agenda. What's essential, however, is for the leader to think about and plan the meeting so that the items are addressed according to a schedule. In other words, if the delegates don't have precise timings on their agendas, make sure you have them on yours. This is one of the biggest responsibilities of the meeting leader. Team members will generally expect you to control the agenda. They will usually respect a decision to close a discussion for the purpose of good timekeeping, even if the discussion is still in full flow.

Meeting Attendees

It's often obvious who should attend, but sometimes it isn't. Consider inviting representatives from other departments to your own department meetings. The "outsiders" will often appreciate being asked. It will help their understanding of your issues, and your understanding of theirs. Having guests from internal and external suppliers also helps build relationships and they can often shed new light on difficult issues.

Avoid and resist senior managers and directors of your own company attending your meetings unless you can be sure that their presence will be positive, and certainly not intimidating. Senior people may be quick to criticize without knowing the facts.

Meeting Date

Be sure the date and time you choose causes minimum disruption for all concerned. It's increasingly difficult to gather people for meetings, particularly from different departments or organizations. So take care when finding the best date. That's a very important part of the process, particularly if senior people are involved.

For ongoing meetings that take place on a regular basis, the easiest way to set dates is to agree on them in advance at the first meeting. Everyone can commit there and then. Try to schedule a year's worth of meetings if possible. Then you can circulate and publish the dates, which keeps people aware of them so that no other priorities encroach.

Preplanning meeting dates is one of the keys to controlled, well-organized meetings. Conversely, leaving the dates until later will almost certainly cause inconvenience and confusion. You may need to be firm. Use the inertia method: that is, suggest a date and invite alternative suggestions, rather than initially asking for possibilities

Meeting Times

The best times to start and finish depend on the type and length of the meeting and the attendees' availability. Generally, try to start early, and to finish at the end of the working day. Two-hour meetings in the middle of the day waste a lot of time. Breakfast meetings are often a good idea.

As with other aspects of the meeting arrangements, if in doubt, always ask people what they prefer. Why guess when you can find out what people actually want, especially if the team is mature and prefers to be consulted anyway?

Meeting Venues

Many meetings are relatively informal, held in rooms on-site. But important meetings held off-site at unfamiliar venues very definitely require careful planning of the layout and facilities. Plan the venue according to the situation. Leave nothing to chance.

Certain preparations are essential and should never be left to a hotel staff or event planner unless you trust them completely. As the leader, you must make certain that the venue is correctly prepared. Some aspects of the meeting that you will need to check—or even set up personally—are the following:

- Seating layout

- Dais

- Tables for demonstration items, paperwork, or handouts

- Electricity outlets and extensions

- Heating and lighting controls

- Projection and flip chart equipment and operation

- Reception and catering arrangements

- Backup equipment availability

All of the above and much more can and will go wrong unless you check and confirm. Clarify your needs when you book the venue and then again a few days before the meeting.

For an important meeting, you should also arrive very early to check that everything is in order. Major meetings are difficult enough without having to deal with emergencies. Remember: If anything goes wrong, it's your credibility and reputation that's at stake.

Positioning of seating and tables is important, and for certain types of meetings it's crucial. Make sure the layout is appropriate for the occasion:

- For formal presentations to large groups, seat the audience in rows, preferably with tables, facing the dais.

- For medium-size participative meetings, use a horseshoe seating layout with the chairs facing the leaders' table.

- For small meetings involving debate and discussion, use a rectangular table with the leader at one end.

- Relaxed team meetings for planning and creative sessions can be held lounge style, with sofas and coffee tables.

As the leader of the meeting, your position in relation to the group is important. If you are confident and comfortable and your authority is beyond doubt, you should sit close to the team members or even sit among them. But if you expect challenge or need to control the group, position yourself farther away and clearly at the head of things.

Be sure everyone can see screens and flip charts properly. Actually sit in the chairs to check this. You'll be surprised how poor the view is from certain positions.

Setting up of projectors and screens is important. Try for the perfect rectangular image, which gives a professional, controlled impression, as soon as you start. Experiment with the adjustment of the projector and the screens. For smaller meetings, a plain white wall is often better than a poor screen.

Position screens and flip charts where they can be used comfortably without obscuring the audience's view. Ensure that the speaker's position is to the side of the screen, not in front of it. Supply plenty of additional flip chart easels and paper, or whiteboard acetates and pens.

In older venues, lighting may be problematic. If there are strong lights above the screen that cannot be switched off independently, these may need to be temporarily disconnected. If you're in a hotel, always ask for help from the maintenance staff rather doing this yourself. And always show your appreciation for the staff. You need them on your side.

Meeting Agenda

The agenda is the tool with which you control the meeting. Include all relevant information. You can avoid the pressure for "any other business" at the end of the meeting if you circulate a draft agenda in advance of the meeting, and ask for any other items for consideration. ("Any other business" often creates a free-for-all session that wastes time and gives rise to new tricky expectations, which if not managed properly will close the meeting on a negative note.)

Formal agendas for board meetings and committees will normally have an established, fixed format that will apply to every meeting. For less formal meetings, concentrate on practicality. Explain the purpose of each item on the agenda. Assign a time frame for all the items. If you have guest speakers or presenters, name them on the agenda. Plan coffee breaks and a lunch break if relevant, and be sure the caterers are informed. In addition to these formal times off, you should allow breaks every hour so that team members can maintain their concentration.

Leading the Meeting

The key to success is keeping control. You can exert this control by sticking to the agenda, managing the relationships and personalities, and concentrating on outcomes. Meetings must have a purpose, and every item covered must have a purpose. Remind yourself and the group of the required outcomes and steer the proceedings toward generating progress, not hot air.

Politely restrain overenthusiastic team members and encourage hesitant ones. Take notes as you go, recording decisions and agreed actions. Include names, measurable outcomes, and deadlines. Do not try to record everything word for word, and if you find yourself leading a particularly talkative group that produces reams of notes and very little else, then change things. Concentrate on achieving the outcomes you set for the meeting when you drew up the agenda. Avoid hurrying decisions if your aim was simply discussion and involvement of team members. But also avoid hours of discussion if you simply need a decision.

Defer new issues to a later time. Simply say, "You may have a point, but it's not for this meeting—we'll discuss it another time."

If you don't know the answer to a question, be honest about this. Don't waffle. State that you'll get back to everyone with the answer at the next meeting, or append it to the meeting notes.

If someone persistently insists on a specific issue that is not on the agenda, bounce it back to him or her with a deadline to report back any findings and recommendations to you.

Look for signs of fatigue, exasperation, confusion, or boredom in attendees and take the necessary action.

Meetings Notes or Minutes

As the leader, you should take the notes yourself unless the meeting format dictates a formal secretary. When you are seen taking the notes, two things happen. First, people respect you for not forcing them to do it. Second, they see you are recording agreed upon actions, so there's no denying or escaping them.

Meeting notes are essential for managing actions and outcomes. They also cement agreements and clarify confusions. A meeting without notes is almost always a waste of time. Actions that go unrecorded are soon forgotten because there's no published record.

After the meeting, copy the notes to all attendees and to anyone else who should have them. The notes should be brief but also precise and clear. Include relevant facts, figures, accountabilities, actions, and time frames. Any planned actions must be clearly described, naming the person or persons responsible, with a deadline. Use the acronym SMART: Specific, Measurable, Attainable, Results oriented, Time phased.

A crucial final element is following up on the agreed actions—your own included. If you run a great meeting, issue great notes, and then fail to see that the actions are completed, your credibility is lost. You must follow up agreed actions and hold people to them. If you don't, if they learn that they can ignore their agreements, your leadership will be fundamentally undermined. By following up, on the other hand, you will encourage team members to respond and perform. Future meetings will benefit, and so will your organization as a whole.

ACTION STEPS

1. Organizational leaders generally have a subtler presence than inspirational leaders do. Are you more of an

organizational leader or an inspirational one? On a scale from one to ten, rate your need to be acknowledged and in the spotlight (one is "very little need," and ten is "I have a great need to be in the spotlight").

| 1 | 2 | 3 | 4 | 5 | 6 | 7 | 8 | 9 | 10 |

Very little   *A great need*

2. Describe three specific steps that you can take toward creating a greater sense of unity among your colleagues (or even among your family and friends). This may involve planning a group event, such as a picnic or a trip to an educational or inspirational location. It may be putting your logo on some T-shirts and caps. Be creative!

3. Are there individuals in your organization who are not team players and need to be personally singled out for their efforts? What steps could you take to acknowledge them for the work that they do, while encouraging them to integrate themselves more as part of the team? Write down three options, and then act upon them.

Let the other person save face.

—Dale Carnegie

CHAPTER 12

The Tactics of Great Organizational Leaders

I n the previous chapter we focused on the principles and tactics of organizational leadership. Now let's look at a leader and a company where those ideas have been put into practice with outstanding results.

SOUTHWEST AIRLINES

Herb Kelleher cofounded Southwest Airlines in 1967, where he held the esteemed position of chairman and CEO for more than forty years. Every aspect of his company was built on a horizontal, democratic model, both for the customers and the employees. This is one organization in which the pyramid has been rendered flat as a pancake.

Southwest Airlines relies almost exclusively on a single type of plane, the Boeing 737, which simplifies maintenance and reduces the need for spare parts inventory. For the customers, there is no first class and there are no seat assignments, but there is an industry-leading record of on-time departures and arrivals. On top of that, Southwest employees enjoy a corporate culture that is intentionally democratic.

Employees even participate in hiring decisions. Once technical skills have been assessed, current employees report on how well the job applicant seems to fit into the team. Team members spend hours with each applicant in casual but revealing conversation about sports, family, or current events. The goal is to find people who are service-oriented and idealistic. Attitude and commitment are the most important factors in a hiring decision. Skills can be taught or augmented if need be.

It's also important to have a sense of humor. The atmosphere there is fun-loving and unpretentious. Prospective team members must be comfortable with that. Kelleher himself likes to laugh. He strongly believes that you shouldn't have to change your personality when you come to work, and he's appeared at company events in costumes ranging from Elvis to the Easter bunny.

Once, a group of pilots came in for job interviews. As the applicants arrived for their appointments, they were told that formal business attire during the interview would not be acceptable. Instead, they'd have to wear a pair of Southwest Airline shorts. So each applicant found himself wearing the shorts along with his dress shirt, tie, and jacket. Those that did not see the humor in this would clearly not fit in at Southwest, regardless of their technical qualifications. They were not hired because compatibility with the organizational culture was the all-important requirement.

Herb Kelleher says things that many other organizational leaders say, but few live up to. He says that leadership by example is crucial. He says that true leadership is actually servanthood, and that the best organizational leaders have to be good followers. They must be able to accept other people's ideas even when those ideas conflict with their own. They have to be willing to place their own ego needs beneath the needs of the organization. Above all, they have to respect the needs of team members and do everything possible to satisfy them.

DOWNSIZING

In terms of organizational leadership, it's this last point that distinguishes the true master. During the '80s and '90s a tremendous upheaval occurred in American business when leaders began drastically cutting workforces in an effort to boost bottom lines. Downsizing was the word for it. This had enormous impact at all levels of society—an impact still being felt.

It also gave rise to a personal style among some corporate leaders of almost gleeful disregard for the human cost of downsizing. Very few of the most unrepentant downsizers still hold power today, which is no surprise to Herb Kelleher. He believes the success of Southwest Airlines is directly connected to the fact that there have never been any furloughs or layoffs. The airline industry is highly competitive, very cyclical, and often chaotic. Kelleher's leadership was based on the principle that team members would be part of the company for a very long time.

Kelleher believed that if they didn't feel secure and confident about that from the moment they were hired, their commitment would diminish. Their customer service would go down, and ultimately the strength of the organization will suffer.

In an interview, former CEO Herb Kelleher remarked on the number of leaders who study Southwest Airlines with an eye to establishing a similar business environment and business model. Yet Kelleher does not really have a formal method or a well-established set of procedures. It is simply a matter of hiring people who will do their best for the customers and for their fellow team members. Visiting executives find this hard to believe. They want a doctrine. They seek out a complex system of dos and don'ts, yet Kelleher feels that anything like that would ruin the organization.

Enrollment

Dale Carnegie, a natural teacher, liked to use the word *enrollment* to describe the relationship between leaders and employees in the creation of a successful organization. Mr. Carnegie believed that leaders must offer their team members the chance to improve themselves, just as a university offers new skills to students who choose to enroll. Team members, by their own choice and for their own benefit, enroll in the strategy, tactics, and principles of the leader. This does not necessarily have to happen at the moment of hiring, but the leader must see the potential for it to happen sooner rather than later.

Enrollment requires focused effort and continual reinforcement. There are no shortcuts. Masters of organizational leadership do not dictate: They enroll. As one CEO explained, "If you enroll one person, then you have the start of a chain reaction. You've changed someone and that person enrolls someone else or maybe two people or maybe ten. They become able to enroll a hundred more."

This is like an old cowboy movie where the hero is going to have the final battle against the villain and rescue the heroine. The hero rides out on his white horse, and then all of a sudden there's a guy next to him. Then there's another guy on the other side, and then ten more on the left. Ten more appear on the right, and a minute later there are hundreds of guys riding by his side. The dust is flying and they're on their way. This did not happen because the guy in the white hat made a phone call and said, "Can you meet me by the creek at ten o'clock in the morning for the big gunfight?" It happened because the cowboy decided to go to the creek himself if need be. When people saw him do that, they wanted to ride along.

A GOOD LEADER CREATES A SENSE OF UNITY

It is the leader's job to create those feelings, the sense that we are in this together. Leaders need to instill a sense that all are part of a team, and that each and every contributor is important. They should encourage the team, enforcing that "Together we'll get it done." Yes, everyone has bills to pay and everyone wants a pay-check. Perhaps everyone also wants a year-end bonus, and a great benefits package. A strong organization, based on real leadership, will never flow from financial incentives alone, nor will it grow using intimidation on employees who have a fear of being fired.

People who work for a paycheck will only work as hard as it takes to get paid. If enough people start thinking that way, noth-ing much is going to get done. A strong organizational leader recognizes people, includes them, encourages them, trains them, asks their opinions, praises them, and empowers them to make decisions. A wise leader shares the glory with them, seeks their advice, makes them understand how valued they are, encourages them to take risks, gives them the freedom to work as they see fit, and then conveys belief in their abilities by getting out of the way. At its best, organizational leadership evolves by showing people that you trust, respect, and care about them.

Great inspirational leaders have the ability to make people fol-low them. This is a unique gift, and even a form of genius. The gift of the organizational leader, however, is subtler and just as great. It requires the ability to get people moving forward. The movement comes, not because of the person leading them, but because they are leading themselves.

WHO ARE WE? WHAT ARE WE?

Each organization has its own distinctive culture. This is a com-bination of the influences of the original founders, the past and present leadership, crises, events, history, and profitability, and much more. It all adds up to the routines, rituals, and "the way we do things here." These behaviors shape the way people act within the organization. They clarify what it takes to be in good stand-ing as a team player, and they indicate appropriate behavior for each circumstance.

The culture of an organization is a relatively abstract concept.

The climate, on the other hand, is the feel of the organization on a daily basis—the individual and shared perceptions and attitudes of the organization's members. The culture is the deeply rooted nature of the group, and is a result of long-held formal and informal systems, rules, traditions, and customs. The climate is a short-term setting created by the current leadership. Climate represents the beliefs about the feel of the organization by its members at the present time. This individual perception of the climate comes from what the people believe about the activities that occur every day and even every minute. These activities influence both individual and team motivation and satisfaction, such as:

- How well does the leader clarify the priorities and goals of the organization? "What is expected of us?"

- What is the system of recognition, rewards, and criticism in the organization? "What will happen if I make a mistake?"

- How competent are the leaders? How highly are they regarded by team members?

- Are leaders free to make decisions?

Organizational climate is directly related to the leadership and management style of upper management, based on the values, attributes, skills, actions, and priorities. Another aspect of this is the "ethical climate"—the feel within the organization about the activities that have "right or wrong" content or those aspects of the work environment that constitute ethical behavior. The ethical climate is the feel about whether we are doing things correctly in a moral sense: the feel of whether we behave the way we ought to behave. The behavior and the character of the leader is the most important factor that impacts the climate of an organization.

Culture is a long-term, complex phenomenon. Culture represents the shared expectations and self-image of the organization, the mature values that create tradition or the "way we do things here." Things are done differently in every organization. The collective vision and common folklore that define the institution are a reflection of culture. Individual leaders cannot easily create or change culture because culture is a part of the organization. Culture influences the characteristics of the climate by its effect on the actions and thought processes of the leader. But everything you do as a leader will affect the climate of the organization.

Here are some ideas for creating optimum culture and climate through consensus and collaboration

Reaching Consensus Through Collaboration

Effective teams work closely together to reach consensus or agreement. Consensus requires that each participant agrees on the point being discussed before it becomes a part of the decision. Not every point will meet with everyone's complete approval. Unanimity is not the goal. The ability to use collaboration requires the recognition of and respect for everyone's ideas, opinions, and suggestions. The goal is to have individuals accept a point of view based on logic. When individuals can understand and accept the logic of a differing point of view, you must assume you have reached consensus.

Follow these guidelines for reaching consensus:

- Avoid arguing over individual ranking or position. Present a position as logically as possible.

- Avoid "win-lose" statements. Discard the notion that someone must win.

- Avoid making people change their minds just to avoid conflict and achieve harmony.

- Avoid majority voting, averaging, bargaining, or coin flipping. These do not lead to real consensus. Treat differences of opinion as being indicative of incomplete sharing of relevant information: Keep asking questions.

- Keep the attitude that holding different views is both natural and healthy to a group.

- View any initial agreement as suspect, especially if it happens quickly. Explore the reasons underlying apparent agreement and make sure that members have willingly agreed.

ACTION STEPS

1. Under the leadership of Herb Kelleher, Southwest Airlines created a unified and mutually respectful culture within its organization. Do you treat everyone with mutual dignity and respect? If not, write a list of individuals whom you do not treat this way. Then with some introspection, make note of why you do not treat them with respect. Very often, if something in someone else triggers us, it's because this person has a trait that we struggle to come to terms with within ourselves.

2. Once you have noted why you struggle with that individual, create a plan to shift your perception. Often writing a list of the things that you DO respect in that individual and focusing on those traits can shift your feelings about him or her, and allow you to see him or her in a different light. After doing this exercise, make note of any changes within yourself, the other person, and your relationship.

3. Herb Kelleher claimed that he did not follow any particular system or methodology. Do you? To clarify your own organizational leadership style, write out a statement on how you lead others. What do you look for when hiring new employees? What interpersonal practices do you insist upon within the organization? What kind of incentive or reward program do you follow? What do you do to encourage team building?

4. If you were the cowboy with the white hat, who within your organization (or within your life as a whole) would follow you into battle and why? What have you done to gain their trust, loyalty and admiration? What can you do to enlist even more?

Talk about your own mistakes before criticizing the other person.

—Dale Carnegie

CHAPTER 13

Finding Your Leadership Style

APPLYING WHAT YOU LEARN TO YOURSELF

We have now seen two distinct leadership styles: the inspirational leader and the organizational leader. Let's briefly review them to assist you in your own leadership style.

AN OVERVIEW OF THE INSPIRATIONAL LEADER

From the perspective of those who work closely with inspirational leaders, there is often not a lot of middle ground. The environment these leaders create is exciting and electric. Some people admire their passion and hail them as visionaries. Others are frustrated by their unpredictable nature.

Working with an inspirational leader, even a true master of inspirational leadership, is a bit like taking a roller-coaster ride. Some people are thrilled. It gets their adrenaline going and they want to ride again. Others stagger away vowing, "Never again." Either way, everyone agrees that inspirational leaders have a gift for putting their unique stamp on things.

THE TRAITS OF THE ORGANIZATIONAL LEADER

Organizational leaders are of a different sort altogether. Their effectiveness derives much less from personal dynamics. If inspirational leadership is like a temperamental high-performance sports car, then organizational leadership is more like a well-engineered sedan. Organizational leaders are built to withstand the bumps in the road, and to get good gas mileage for the long haul. They are interested in creating a rock-solid structure, both for the present and for those who will come after them.

Organizational leaders like to see things through to completion. They are good at anticipating obstacles and developing alternative strategies. People describe these sorts of leaders as being on top of things. Unlike the inspirational leader, they often have a tremendous capacity for thinking about detail.

SELF-ASSESSMENT QUESTIONS

Now that you're getting a feel for the different ways leadership masters operate, it's time to take what you've learned and apply it. For the next two chapters, we will take you through a series of self-assessment questions. After you have read this chapter and absorbed the background information on the questions, please go to the action steps section and write your responses to the self-assessment questions in the space provided. At the bottom of each space you'll find information to help you interpret what you've written and to begin identifying your personal leadership style.

As we begin our discussion of the questions, please remember this: Nothing is written in stone. This self-assessment questionnaire is simply a picture of where you are right now. It is an indication of where you stand at this moment in your personal development.

If you don't like the picture, then you've got the power to change it. You have free will, imagination, and the capacity to grow. If you like the picture, you can gain insights to expand on your strengths.

As you consider the questions, there are a few key points to keep in mind. Be honest with yourself, try not to second-guess the questions, and do not answer them in the way you *think* you *should*. This assessment is for your benefit and no one else will see it.

Also, try to avoid brief, generalized answers. Write as much as you can for each response, including circumstances, thoughts, emotions, and people (internal and external details that will flesh out your answer into something useful for you to work with later). The more you write, the more you'll get out of the process. With these things in mind, we're ready to begin.

IMPORTANT QUESTIONS

What Is the Biggest Career or Work-Related Decision You Have Made, and How Did You Make It?

Your experience with making difficult or important decisions has nothing to do with the length of your résumé, nor whether you've ever been interviewed by CNN. No matter where you are in your professional life, whether you're an administrative assistant or a CEO, you've already made some very big career decisions. You may not have realized it. If you have not, it is critical that you do.

This point was made very well by a man named Doyle Brunson, who has won the World Series of Poker in Las Vegas, Nevada, ten times. Once, Brunson was asked about the pressure he felt when he pushed a million dollars' worth of chips into the center of the table on a single bet. "That's not pressure," the gambler replied. "Pressure is when you're betting your last dime."

The importance of any decision is determined by how much it can affect your own life. Smoking a first cigarette may turn out to be a big decision and a very destructive one, though it didn't seem

like much at the time. Seemingly insignificant choices like returning a phone call, answering a letter, or doing a friend a small
favor have transformed more than one person's life. So give this
some real thought. Often the most life-changing choices are really
about changing small details of things we do every day.

Are You a Concept Person or an Execution Person? Provide Your Reasoning or Give an Example for Your Answer.

This is like the difference between a poet and a novelist, or between an inventor and an engineer. A concept person thinks of an
idea like Pet Rocks or Beanie Babies. An execution person knows
just how to price and market them. A concept person sketches
new lines of fashionable clothing each season. An execution person adapts those designs for production, contracts with vendors,
and oversees an ad campaign to promote them.

Concept people see everyday objects with fresh eyes. They
are masters at free association. Their talents are what spark new
trends, inspire innovative products, create fresh approaches, and
cause new services to be born. Execution people play a much
different role. Without them, clever ideas would never manifest
themselves in our daily lives. They fiddle with ideas until they can
be realistically turned into products that hit the shelves at cost
and on time.

Both talents are necessary. Neither could accomplish much
without the existence of the other. Both are potential leadership
masters. Which one are you?

Are You Inspired by Detail or Impatient with It?

Meg, a recent law school graduate, took a trip to Europe before
returning to take the bar exam. While visiting Prague, she found
that walking the streets of an old-world city could be its own

kind of education. On a narrow side street, Meg peered through a window and observed an elderly watchmaker with three young apprentices. Dozens of delicate watch parts were arranged neatly on the table in front of them. There were heaps of tiny coils and springs and bits of metal and delicate crystals for use as watch faces. From time to time, the watchmaker stood up to look at an apprentice's work, but for the most part, the view through the window was one of pure concentration and of people inspired by detail.

Detail-oriented people thrive in situations that allow them to delve into the process of taking things one step at a time with methodical concentration. They find no appeal in a broad, generalized approach to things.

Of course, some people would be climbing the walls instead of patiently disassembling an antique watch. For them, the methodical attention that's required for this kind of effort is boring and may seem pointless. They have the capacity for great commitment and hard work, but when it comes time to dive into the smaller parts of the process, they're already onto the next order of business. Their strengths don't lie in carefully fitting together the smaller pieces of the puzzle, no matter how critical those pieces might turn out to be.

WHAT TYPE OF LEADER ARE YOU?

Are You a Conservative or an Aggressive Leader?

Do you play to win or to prevent yourself from losing? Do you think that the best defense is a good offense, or is it the other way around?

Don't make the mistake of thinking one of these styles is somehow better than the other. On the surface the aggressive thinker might seem like a superior leader, but don't be fooled. Depending upon the circumstances, conservative thinking can save the day.

Imagine that an armed robber has taken hostages in a bank. Time ticks away as the gunman inside the building remains in a standoff with police. The public may be crying out for action, but more often than not, it's the cool-headed, conservative approach that saves the people inside. It may not make for a great movie adaptation, but that matters very little to the families of the hostages who are released unharmed. In this instance it is easy to see that an aggressive move could quickly turn into a violent and needless disaster.

In the business world, however, there are plenty of opportunities for aggressive thinkers to flourish. When America Online announced that it would purchase the giant Time Warner conglomerate, it was easy to forget that, only a few years before, the future of AOL was anything but bright. The hourly fees the company charged for Internet access were drastically undercut by other providers. Customers were leaving AOL in droves. Then, in a move that took everyone by surprise, Steve Case of America Online announced that hourly fees would be abolished, and service would be offered for a single monthly fee, one that in many cases was only a fraction of what people had been paying.

The line of demarcation is clear. Aggressive leaders are not daunted by risks. They are creative strategists and they are often at their best when their backs are against the wall. Conservative leaders limit damage. They anticipate ways to avoid unnecessary losses to protect the larger organization. Different kinds of people have different strengths. Your task now is to discover where your own strengths lie.

Do You Use Your Emotions in Your Work-Related Decision Making?

In other words, do you trust your gut or trust the numbers? When you're faced with a tough choice, do you respond intuitively or analytically?

While it's true that instincts and hard data often work together, when they're at odds, one often trumps the other, depending upon which process makes you most comfortable. When a very successful bond trader left the Chicago Board of Trade to take a position trading natural gas in Houston, it seemed like a step into the unknown. Why would anyone want to leave a career that was providing such success? The bond trader himself found it difficult to explain. "The numbers only tell me so much," he said. "I work on instinct. I don't know any other way to describe it."

Steve Jobs, of Apple Inc., is a similar example of instinctive decision making. When he returned to lead the company he had cofounded, there were serious problems that Apple had never faced before. Sales were dismal. Other brands had caught up with Apple in ease of use, and many were significantly less costly. The numbers were definitely bad, but Jobs remained passionate about Apple. He had faith in its strength as a market innovator, and as a company that had its finger on the consumer pulse. He had strong instincts about what was missing from the home computer market, and the iMac model proved him right. It was small, easy to operate, portable, and fun to look at.

A less emotional approach to decisions is also a valuable approach. For many people the notion that "the numbers don't lie" has served them very well when it comes time to make a tough choice, regardless of what's happening in their gut. What's critical is becoming aware of your own process and identifying your own decision-making priorities.

As a Leader, Do You Try to Build Consensus or Do You Go at It Alone?

Some people hear the word *consensus* and breathe a sigh of satisfaction. Others hear the same word and grit their teeth. Why the different reactions?

Leaders who favor consensus and collaboration consider it the optimal group dynamic. They feel that the rightness of a decision is validated when most of the group agrees with it. It's a harmonizing process. Consensus builders are convinced that going forward as a team will increase an organization's overall effectiveness. Even on a personal level, they're most comfortable in this sort of atmosphere.

Being a consensus builder, however, takes considerable skill and tenacity. It requires knowing how to interact with all sorts of personalities. It means being an astute judge of others. These leaders are tireless negotiators, constantly readjusting their mental balance sheets, while they edge everyone closer to the middle. Like a cat that always lands on its feet, a consensus builder knows how to stay in control while navigating a fluid situation.

In all of American history, the classic consensus builder was President Lyndon B. Johnson. As a senator, he had a reputation as the skilled deal maker. Johnson could get politicians on both sides of the aisle to support a bill or to rally around a cause. That skill served Johnson well when he was elected president. Despite overwhelming opposition from Southern senators, Johnson was able to get the 1964 Civil Rights Act passed by Congress. After many days of grueling debate, America had the most sweeping civil rights act in the country's history.

At this point, you may be wondering, "Who in their right mind would be against consensus?" After all, what could possibly be wrong with everyone being in agreement? But every aspect of leadership has a flip side, an opposite style that can be equally effective.

When Bill Gates of Microsoft holds a business meeting, nothing annoys him more than a room in which all are nodding their heads. Gates believes that consensus often is a sign of lazy or conformist thinking. The best work, in his opinion, comes from confrontation, challenge, and contrarian thinking. "That's the stupidest thing I've ever heard" is a comment Gates has made more than once in a business meeting, just to get the sparks flying.

How would you react to that sort of style? Are you a consensus builder or someone who likes to puncture balloons?

You have now been given six questions that will assist you in assessing exactly what your leadership style is. These questions are reiterated in the action steps below. Be sure to answer each as specifically and completely as possible.

ACTION STEPS

1. Before revisiting the leadership assessment questions, review the list of guidelines for effective leadership below. Put a ✓ by those attributes that you feel you have mastered, and put an X by those that you need to further develop in yourself.

   The effective leader should keep the following guidelines in mind when it is necessary to change attitudes or behavior:

   - Be sincere. Do not promise anything you cannot deliver.

   - Forget about the benefits to yourself and concentrate on the benefits to the other person.

   - Know exactly what it is you want the other person to do.

   - Be empathetic. Ask yourself, "What is it the other person really wants?"

   - Consider the benefits that person will receive from doing what you suggest.

   - Match those benefits to the other person's wants.

- When you make your request, put it in a form that will convey to the other person the idea that he or she, personally, will benefit.

It's naive to believe you will always get a favorable reaction from other persons when you use these approaches, but the experience of most people shows that you are more likely to change attitudes this way than by not using these principles. If you increase your success by even a mere 10 percent, you will become 10 percent more effective as a leader than you were before. And that is your benefit.

2. Answer the following questions, keeping in mind these two points. First, be honest with yourself. This assessment is for your benefit, and no one else will see it. The more honest you are, the more lifelike your verbal snapshot will be. In particular, avoid the temptation of second-guessing yourself to create a "better" answer—because for this exercise, the best answer is the truth, just as it occurs to you.

Second, try to avoid brief, generalized answers. Write as much as you can for each response, including circumstances, thoughts, emotions, and people. Include internal and external details that will flesh your answer into something useful for you to work with later. The more you write, the more you'll get out of the process.

1. What is the biggest career or work-related decision you have made, and how did you make it?

2. Are you a concept person or an execution person? Please explain your answer.

3. Are you inspired by detail or impatient with it? Provide examples for your answer.

4. Are you a conservative or an aggressive leader? Why do you say that?

5. Do you use your emotions in your work-related decision making? Give specific examples.

6. As a leader, do you try to build consensus or do you go at it alone? Please explain.

There is only one way under high heaven to get the best of an argument—and that is to avoid it.

—Dale Carnegie

CHAPTER 14

Continuing to Discover Your Leadership Style

The last question in chapter 13 dealt with whether you are a consensus builder or prefer to make decisions alone. One leadership style may be just as effective as another, depending on the organization and specifics of the situation. While Bill Gates cringes at the thought of consensus in a business, the following account shows how employee involvement and decision making on a large scale can also benefit an organization.

PEOPLE WANT TO MAKE AN IMPACT

A large corporation in the home products industry discovered exactly how employee involvement could benefit all those involved. As part of an attempt to revitalize the downtown area of the company's home city, a new plant was being built in a previously run-down area. People were hired from the same area and training and orientation were expected to take time. Nonetheless, the company committed itself to involving the employees and residents on important issues concerning the new plant.

This involvement led to the rerouting of public transportation closer to the plant, an expanded day care facility, and greater flexibility in hiring and job classification. For many community residents, discussing these issues with representatives of a major corporation was a totally new experience. It had proved to be a valuable one for both them and the company. For the company it was a chance to build loyalty and commitment in a demographic base from which the majority of new hires would be drawn. For the workers there was the realization that the new employer wanted their ideas and that those ideas would be acted upon at the top levels. It ended up being a winning solution for all involved.

Making that happen requires vision and flexibility. The chief operating officer of the home products company describes empowering his employees as one of his most important jobs. It's also a very complex one. It involves instilling confidence in team members and bringing out their creativity. It also requires helping them clarify their own thoughts so that they can be communicated to people who may have very different cultural expectations.

One executive says, "I've learned something that I would never have understood a few years ago. There really is no such thing as a wrong or an irrelevant thought. Literally everyone's ideas deserve to be thrown into the stew. That's the only way you'll come up with solutions that are really workable, solutions that are not only technically sound but inclusive of all the people who will carry them out."

LOOKING AT CONFRONTATION

We will now continue to provide you with additional questions to assist you in your self-assessment. Again, take the time to answer these questions with as much detail as possible.

How Do You Feel About Confrontation?

This question is really an extension of the previous one, but it deals more with one-on-one, individual relationships. As a leader, do you see yourself as a straight shooter or a diplomat? Do people describe you as "easygoing and a team player" or do they use words like "frank, direct, and blunt"?

Looking back on conflict situations, some leaders believe that they have failed by just letting things go that far. Others have fond memories of their confrontations, of not backing down, of speaking out, and of asserting control.

So, ask yourself: Do you see confrontation as a breakdown of leadership or as a fundamental expression of it?

Are You a Scientist or a Magician?

This question is really about the importance you assign to consistency. How much weight do you give to tried-and-true formulas? Are you most comfortable sticking with what has worked in the past or do you like to see things happen in unexpected ways?

The test of a scientific approach is its ability to predict the future. Based on past experience, we can expect that dropping a stone will result in its falling toward the ground. This is the law of gravity in action and it's proven very accurate in predicting the results of certain actions. As a scientific theory, it is always subject to testing and verification. As strange as it may seem, apparently immutable natural laws are only as good as their last example. If we drop that stone and it doesn't fall to the ground, even once, everything is up for grabs. At least in that situation, the law of gravity hasn't worked, which should lead to a reevaluation and possibly a revision of some fundamental concepts.

Magic, on the other hand, doesn't have to work all the time to still be magical. The magician believes that all the variables in a situation can never be known and that even the force of his or her own belief and that of the onlookers can influence an outcome. Each new effort has its own dynamic, its own set of unpredictable factors that make it a universe unto itself. A wonderful scene in the film *Little Big Man* illustrates this. Playing a tribal chief, the actor Dan George turns to costar Dustin Hoffman, and says that it is time for him to die. He wants to say good-bye. It is a sad and touching moment. He lies down, closes his eyes, and prepares for death. There's a minute of silence. Finally the old man asks, "Am I still in this world?" Hoffman's character replies, "Yes, Grandfather." The chief sits up and shrugs his shoulders, saying, "Sometimes the magic works. Sometimes it doesn't."

If this is your style, sticking closely to track records feels like an unnecessary constraint. Things don't have to work every time to be true or worth believing in. You like to have an element of mystery in your life, even in major business decisions. When Michael Ovitz was the most powerful agent in Hollywood, he hired world-renowned architect I. M. Pei to design new headquarters for Creative Artists Agency. The cost was many millions of dollars and Ovitz was known as a careful manager of funds. He also made sure, however, that the construction of the new building conformed to the principles of the ancient Chinese spiritual tradition known as feng shui. Even in the very unmystical environment of Hollywood deal making, decisions were made outside the limits of pure reason.

If your leadership style is to look closely at what's tried and true, you're probably closer to the scientist in your orientation. You pay attention to the accumulated data. You study past outcomes as a way of predicting future success.

If you, instead, find yourself wanting to try things that can't really be quantified or verified, you need to have some magic in your approach to leadership.

How Do You Regard Your Competitors?

For the purposes of this question, the word *competitors* refers to people who are both inside and outside your organization. It may refer to someone at your same level in a company, or it may refer to another company that produces the same product or service as yours. In any case, how you see your competitors is a key indicator of your leadership style.

Specifically, do you see your competitors as opponents in battle, or do you see them as basically people like yourself who are doing the best job they can? Do you see them as influential peers who can even help to bring out the best in you through their efforts?

Martin, for example, was a very successful manufacturer of children's clothing. His clients were large department stores. His line was always top quality and designed to be shipped on time. He had few problems with returns and buyers came back to him season after season.

Meanwhile, Stan, a competitor in the children's clothing business, hated the very mention of Martin's company. He didn't want to hear about Martin's latest line, or about which store was carrying what. For him, such talk was treason. It made his blood pressure go up just to think about the success Martin was having, even though Martin certainly worked to earn it.

David, a third party in the same industry, saw things quite differently. A newcomer to that business, he quickly saw that Martin was someone to watch if he ever hoped to be a success himself. David made a habit of visiting department stores and specialty shops to study the type of product Martin sent out each season. During meetings with buyers, who also worked with Martin, he asked them what they liked about his competitor and what they didn't like. He saw Martin not as an enemy, but as a catalyst for challenging himself.

A few years later, at a garment industry awards dinner, a buyers' association honored David. He stood up to acknowledge the award and express his gratitude to the people he worked with. Then he paused and took a moment to thank Martin himself for showing him the way it should really be done. Stanley, of course, was floored. To him, David's behavior was deeply irrational. To the award-winner, David, however, it made perfect sense.

How does it seem to you?

WHAT WOULD YOU LIKE PEOPLE TO SAY ABOUT YOU?

How Do You Feel About Grooming a Successor?

For some people in leadership positions, and even for some who could unquestionably be called leadership masters, the idea that they will let go of the reins at some point seems very threatening. They prefer not to engage in that kind of thinking. Some teachers don't like hearing about how great the substitute did in their absence. Some people don't like the idea of making out a will, even though on another level they know it's an advisable and prudent thing to do. After all, grooming a successor is not only about the effort of finding and preparing the appropriate candidate; it touches on the idea that we are not indispensable. This realization clashes with the way certain leaders run their organizations.

For example, when Disney's Michael Eisner underwent heart bypass surgery, stockholders suddenly noticed that little had been done to groom a successor for Eisner, should one become necessary. Eisner quickly returned to work and continued to give little attention to who might come after him. Obviously, it was something that made him uncomfortable. Part of his leadership style was the idea that there would be no looking beyond it.

Other leaders don't find this issue at all unsettling. In fact, they regard it as an important part of their responsibility. It is considered part of ensuring the future of the organization. In their eyes, along with the larger group stability, they feel that their own efforts and victories will be protected when such transitions are prepared and implemented without difficulty. As you respond to this question, ask yourself how you feel about the eventual relinquishing of leadership. Do you see it as another opportunity, or an unpleasant necessity? Is it perhaps something that you don't even want to think about?

If You Could Eavesdrop on a Conversation About Your Leadership, What Would You Most Want to Hear?

This final question is perhaps the most revealing of all. If you could eavesdrop on a conversation that complimented or described you in some way, what is the one thing you'd most appreciate? Would it be that you're a team player? Would you like to be considered tough but fair? Would it please you to be described as passionate about your work, good with your staff, and approachable and easy to talk to? The choices are endless. You will need to give this some real thought. Take the time to do so. You might even like to write your answer to this question in the form of an imaginary dialogue. The insights can be very rewarding and it's fun to imagine a conversation in which you hear nothing but good things about yourself.

This concludes our self-assessment process. Now, please complete the corresponding section in your action steps. When you're done, read over your responses. This will take you a long way toward discovering whether you're basically an inspirational leader, an organizational one, or perhaps in transition toward a clear personal style.

Remember, this is a snapshot, not a stone sculpture intended to endure for all time. Like the world around you, you're a work in progress. The purpose of this exercise is to give you an accurate take on where you are right now.

ACTION STEPS

Continue your self-assessment by answering the following questions. Again, keep in mind that, for the best results, first, be honest with yourself, and second, try to avoid brief, generalized answers. Write as much as you can for each response, including circumstances, thoughts, emotions, and people—internal and external details that will flesh your answer into something useful for you to work with later. The more you write, the more you'll get out of the process.

1. How do you feel about confrontation? Explain in detail.

2. Are you a scientist or a magician? What makes you say that?

3. How do you regard your competitors? Provide specific examples.

4. How do you feel about grooming a successor?

5. If you could eavesdrop on a conversation about your leadership, what would you most want to hear?

Consistently high performance comes from a balance of work and leisure.

—Dale Carnegie

CHAPTER 15

Leadership in Balance I: Whole Health

Let's begin this chapter by making an observation that may surprise you. It has to do with the limits of leadership success or, rather, with the fact that real success should have no limits. We've all heard of people who have achieved great things in their careers. We have all heard of individuals who have become successful entrepreneurs or the heads of big companies, but their personal lives are in chaos. Their families have broken up, they have damaged their health, or they never seem able to take a moment away from work.

These people are not leadership masters because they have failed to lead themselves effectively in the most important areas of their lives. In fact, part of the problem might be some confusion about what's really important, and what's less important, about what the means and what the ends are. These people may be so obsessed with reaching certain goals that they lose track of their core values.

"I don't think it's possible to be a great manager or a great executive without being a total person," says the president of an international computer systems company. "You can be a good executive and make money for your company, but if you don't get along with your spouse and your children, you're missing a crucial part of life.

Someone once said, "No matter what you've done for yourself or for humanity, if you can't look back on having given love and attention to your own family, what have you really accomplished?" Actually the person who said that wasn't just "someone." It was Lee Iacocca, the former CEO of Chrysler Corporation. He was referring to the need for perspective or leadership mastery in all areas of our lives. In the next few pages, we will explore tactics and techniques for helping you attain that balance. Surprisingly, when this is achieved, it will actually generate renewed energy and focus for your career.

SYNERGY

You may be familiar with a word that describes this process. The word is *synergy*. It refers to the interaction of two or more forces so that their combined effect is greater than the sum of their individual effects. In everyone's life the two major forces are the desires for professional fulfillment and for personal fulfillment. And they are synergistic. Success at one can or should foster success in the other.

In this chapter, our approach to achieving balance will come in two parts. We'll first discuss how to strengthen your resources and develop a balanced perspective. Then we will address how all this can be applied to everyday life. It's a dual process: training and performance, along with learning and application.

The chairman of a nationally prominent public relations firm once observed that "A successful life needs to have many dimensions for your family, your friends, your personal pastimes, and your health." Right now, how happy are you with these dimensions in your life? Many of us are not really accustomed to thinking about them. Maybe they are subjects that you prefer to avoid altogether, but discipline is needed here. It's a new kind of discipline, but it is an important aspect of leadership mastery. It is a willingness to look at who we really are and to ask, "Is this who I really want to be?" If the answer is "No," then you've got some work to do. In fact, you've got some work to do even if the answer is "Not exactly" or "Not quite yet." Remember, success is not success unless it's complete. It is not mastered unless it encompasses all areas of your experience.

We can be more specific. A truly balanced life requires, first of all, a certain level of good physical health. Are the ways you eat, sleep, and exercise moving you in the direction you want to go or in the opposite direction? At the headquarters of a worldwide money management firm in New York City, a fully equipped workout room has been built right outside the president's office. All employees are encouraged to use it. In fact, the president of the firm intends to see the workout room triple in size. He says, "I like to see people come here after work instead of going to health clubs all over the city. They are talking with each other and exchanging ideas, which is good for everyone."

Getting into Shape

Getting into shape does not suggest that you have to train for a marathon. It does involve doing something that's physically active. Many studies have shown that even a brisk walk around the block three times a week is a huge benefit compared to doing nothing at all. So, you can begin moderately, but with a firm commitment to sticking to your goals. Billy Blanks is the Tae Bo master who parlayed his karate championships and personal charisma into an exercise empire. He advises beginners to stand up straight and tell themselves they can be conquerors. And it works.

Negative thinking and discouragement saps your energy before you begin. It's like the mental equivalent of carrying a fifty-pound load on your back. As you progress, you can increase your level of activity. At the beginning, however, keep in mind that just twelve minutes of exercise, four times a week, is all it takes to set you on the right road. That is less than an hour every seven days, the equivalent of watching a weekly sitcom.

Proper Rest

Just as fitness and activity are crucial for personal leadership mastery, so is proper rest. Americans are working harder than ever before. This may be fine, but they're also sleeping worse than ever. This combination of a longer workday and less rest time can be a recipe for disaster. A recent study revealed a direct correlation between reduced hours of sleep and physical aging. A sleep-deprived thirty-year-old, for example, may outwardly look his age but his body may be functioning like someone fifteen years older.

More specifically, you may identify yourself as a morning person or a night person, but this can be self-deluding. Consider this: For thousands of years no one even knew what a night person was. There was no electric light. There were no twenty-four-hour coffee shops or late-night infomercials. People rose when the sun rose and went to sleep when darkness fell. The obligation to feed animals, do time-consuming domestic chores, hunt, or farm plots of land made going to bed early and getting enough sleep a matter of survival. Interestingly, with this full schedule, people were free from many of the most dangerous health issues that burden modern society. Until the start of the twentieth century, many doctors saw very few heart attacks or cases of cardiovascular disease. This was partly because people gave their hearts a rest at night.

Some recent studies of sleep habits can help with this. Researchers have determined an invisible cutoff line that separates two distinct sleep behaviors. That line occurs at ten o'clock at night. There are people whose sleep habits position them on either side: those who go to bed before ten and those who stay up much later. So, if you are in the second category, try making some adjustments. If you still have work to do at night, it's better to rise early in the morning than to stay up toiling past midnight.

What if you simply can't sleep? First, make sure that you and your doctor rule out any medical factor that might disturb your sleep patterns. Consider whether recent or frequent travel has upset your internal clock. Often, particularly among business travelers, the body's rhythms get out of whack from trying to adjust to different time zones, until you feel as if you're permanently in the twilight zone.

If you wake up frequently during the night, there may be something you feel you've left undone. So try to identify what that might be. Dale Carnegie himself recognized this principle. "If you can't sleep," he advised, "then get up and do something instead of lying there and worrying."

Sufficient rest and consistent exercise need to be fundamental components of our lives. A software executive in Palo Alto, California, commented, "I'm not exactly a staple on the late-night social circuit. In fact, I go to bed at 9:30 every night. Now, this amuses my wife and mildly embarrasses my teenage daughter. But I honestly believe anything I may have accomplished professionally has been because I sleep early and get up early. While the other guy is shutting off his alarm clock, I've already had my first good idea of the day."

Nutrition and a Balanced Diet

We all need maintenance and we all need to refuel. It is not just severe illness or major accidents that take their toll on a human being. As with an automobile or any other piece of machinery, normal wear and tear can have long-term effects.

One of the ways to prevent anything beyond normal wear and tear is to maintain a healthy and well-balanced diet. Do you eat breakfast each day? Do you get enough fiber, fruits, vegetables, and protein in your diet? Do you often skip meals? Do you take supplements regularly? We are often guilty of running on empty throughout the day, frequently when we are busiest and most in need of fuel.

Just as parents are advised to put their own oxygen masks on before attending to their child during airplane emergencies, effective leaders need to be sure that they take proper care of themselves before they attempt to care for others in their organization. While skipping meals during a busy day may seem like a short-term gain, this can have a negative long-term effect on you as a leader, and on the bottom line of your business. Your mind needs to be sharp and clear. Without proper care, it will dull.

Since the effects of wear and tear accumulate gradually, they might be hard to spot. Proper nutrition and exercise are imperative to effective leadership. If you take care of your car, you should devote at least as much attention to your own physical and emotional well-being.

RELAXATION AND TIME AWAY

Besides keeping in good physical condition and developing healthy lifestyle habits, there should be times when you completely get away from your work and just relax. For people in demanding leadership roles, a vacation isn't just an indulgence. It is a necessity. It provides you with an opportunity to reset your internal clock, see new places, and make new friends. Most important, a vacation can be an opportunity to reconnect with the people most important to you. It doesn't have to be weeks at the seashore. Even a quick weekend trip can be an effective strategy for rejuvenation.

INTELLECTUAL AND CREATIVE BALANCE

So far, we've been talking about creating balance physically and emotionally. It is equally important to stimulate yourself intellectually and perhaps even artistically, if you're so inclined. Education is a process that should never stop. In fact, unfortunately for many people, real education doesn't even begin until they're in their middle years.

For a leader, learning should have a definition far beyond what takes place in formal schooling. You can learn from everyone. You can learn from everything. It doesn't need to have an obvious application to your career.

Gaining a better understanding of American history, visiting an art museum, or even reading a trade journal from outside your industry will enhance your interactions with other people both at home and at work. When was the last time you were inside your local library? A prominent trial attorney in San Francisco takes home four books a month and reads them, but he doesn't look at the titles before checking them out. By picking books at random he's developed knowledge of philosophy, history, fiction, and even higher mathematics. Sooner or later these have all helped him in his work. More important, they helped him feel that his world is continuously expanding, instead of getting smaller and smaller with each passing year. The Chinese have a saying, "After three days without reading, talk becomes flavorless." Many very bright people would say the same thing about life.

CULTIVATING YOUR SPIRIT

Just as the intellect needs to be cultivated, so does the spirit. This does not necessarily mean formal religious observance, although many people make that choice. Spiritual awareness is very important. The reasons may be difficult to express in numbers or words, but there's no arguing with the abundance of personal evidence.

In the late eighteenth century, there was a mutiny on the HMS *Bounty*, a former British collier that had been outfitted for a botanical expedition in the South Pacific. Captain William Bligh and eighteen crew members who remained loyal to him were set adrift in a small boat. Their boat could carry only meager supplies of food and water, while the men remaining on the *Bounty* had full provisions. Although the small boat sailed for weeks, there was no loss of life on it, and, miraculously, morale remained high. The captain demanded the strict rationing of food and water. He also began and ended each day with prayers and readings from the Bible. In fact, after they were finally rescued, both he and his men attributed their survival to the attention they had given to spiritual needs, as if the food and water were less important. It's interesting to note that the mutineers, who stayed with the ship, quickly degenerated into discord and violence.

You may not feel as if you've been set adrift in a small boat, or maybe you do feel that way sometimes. In any case, you have a spiritual dimension that needs to be respected and developed. For many people who do this, the benefits are very clear. They have fewer stress-related health problems, suffer less from anxiety and other psychological disorders, and in general seem to be immune from feelings of despair and loneliness. These are the facts. Use them to your benefit. Make time in your life for a spiritual dimension.

In fact, time itself is the key element in a balanced lifestyle. We will look at that issue more closely in the next chapter.

ACTION STEPS

1. At the beginning of this chapter, we discussed balance in all aspects of your life as a leader. On a scale from one to ten (one being very unhappy, and ten being extremely happy), rate your happiness in the following areas of your life:

Family:

1   2   3   4   5   6   7   8   9   10

Very unhappy   *Extremely happy*

Friends:

1   2   3   4   5   6   7   8   9   10

Very unhappy   *Extremely happy*

Personal Pastimes:

1   2   3   4   5   6   7   8   9   10

Very unhappy   *Extremely happy*

Overall Health:

1   2   3   4   5   6   7   8   9   10

Very unhappy   *Extremely happy*

Now review each scale, and list at least three things that you can do to improve your rating in each category.

2. Balance in the area of your physical well-being is also required if you wish to be a truly fulfilled leader. Rate your state of health in the following areas, then make the necessary changes to improve your rating in each area:

Sleep:

1   2   3   4   5   6   7   8   9   10

Not enough   *Very well rested*

Exercise:

1   2   3   4   5   6   7   8   9   10

Do very little   *Exercise regularly*

Nutrition:

1   2   3   4   5   6   7   8   9   10

Very unhealthy diet   *Excellent diet*

3. Earlier in this chapter we mentioned a prominent trial attorney who takes home four books a month from the library and reads them. The trick is that he does not look at the titles before checking them out. This gives him a breadth of knowledge in a myriad subjects. Make a point of trying this yourself. Set a date and time, and at least once check out four random books from the library and read them. Make note of any insights or knowledge that you gain from doing so.

4. Following some kind of spiritual practice or principles in your life proves to enhance it. With the massive responsibilities that leadership masters face on a constant basis, they often find greater ease in their lives when they have some basis of faith and trust. Have you incorporated a spiritual dimension into your life? Write three steps that you can take to further cultivate it.

Above all, be constructive.

—Dale Carnegie

CHAPTER 16

Leadership in Balance II: Time and Family

We discussed physical health in the previous chapter. Taking proper care of your mind, body, and spirit is essential to leadership mastery. Two other elements of total health need to be addressed: time and family. You may eat well and exercise regularly, but if you constantly feel that you are in a rush and don't have enough time in the day, stress can erase all your efforts. Similarly, having spiritual fulfillment in your life without the joy of intimate familial relationships would not complete the circle of balance in your life. Making peace with time and creating vital connections with your loved ones are also essential ingredients to optimum personal health and well-being.

TIME: YOUR MOST VALUABLE RESOURCE

Time is really the most valuable resource a leader has. It's also one of the most challenging and the most interesting. For one thing, no matter what your net worth or annual income or job title, you have exactly the same amount of time as everyone else. Not a minute more and not a minute less. Good time management is simply the art of using each twenty-four hours as effectively as possible.

Whether we're trying to build an effective organization, plan a vacation, or build a successful marriage, hurry seems to be a common condition. It happens at all ages and income levels. Students juggle homework and part-time jobs. Parents struggle with the competing demands of career and child-rearing. Today, many people even find themselves doubly pressed for time: caring for aging parents while also trying to raise a family. The following simple guidelines can serve as a starting point for reorganizing your time, if you find it keeps getting away from you. Feel free to add your own successful methods for getting the most out of the time you have available. You will find action steps to help you with this at the end of this chapter.

Use an Organizer or Day Planner

First, get into the habit of using an organizer or day planner of some kind. Keep it with you so that changes in schedules or ongoing commitments can be recorded right away. Then sit down at least once a week and see where your time is actually going. Pay particular attention to the way in which you spend the hours that you are not at work.

Second, avoid energy-draining, time-wasting black holes. Watching television is probably the most common example. While TV can be relaxing or educational, it can also steal precious hours better used for something else. If you're a habitual watcher, use your organizer to determine how much time you're actually spending in front of the screen. Then make a plan for reducing your TV time to a minimum.

Third, be realistic about what you can accomplish in the time you have. Overreaching, beyond what you can possibly get done, can keep you stuck in a permanent time crunch. Even if you apply every skill you've learned in this program, you can still encounter problems by scheduling ten hours of activity in seven hours of time. For many people, a key step is learning to say "no" to additional obligations whenever possible.

Next, remember this important principle, "When it comes to being organized, every little bit helps." Chaos wastes time. Order restores it. As you begin implementing a time management program, start small and keep at it. Identify three or four problem areas at home and at work. Then commit fifteen minutes to addressing those specific problems, even if it takes you a week or a month. Don't go on to anything else until those issues are resolved.

Fifth, make your downtime count. There are moments of un-committed time in everyone's day. They may not be more than a few minutes, but you can use them to chip away at things that need to be done. Waiting in a doctor's office and sitting at the car wash are cases in point. By using just ten minutes a day more efficiently, you can add a few hours to your schedule over the course of a week.

A final point about time management concerns the concept of synergy that we discussed earlier. All of the ways you develop the qualities of a leader in your personal life work together.

You don't manage your time in a vacuum. When you're fit, full of energy, and sleeping well, for example, you will find time management to be much easier. Ultimately, this chapter on creating balance is about one simple principle. It's about being in control of your own life and not letting it control you.

FAMILY

We've been talking a lot about how to strengthen your resources. Now let's examine the settings in which these resources are called upon in your personal life. For most people, this begins with family. That can mean a spouse and children, although increasingly this traditional model of family is only one piece of a much larger picture of how people live.

So when we discuss family, keep in mind that it embraces all the models of what family can mean: single-parent families, unmarried people, extended family, one child, many children, or a group of close friends that functions like a familial support system. How your own family is structured is less important than the time and care you invest in it.

Family is our most important organizational unit. While blood ties are inherently powerful, you get from a family what you put into it. This is true of parenting, of marriage, and of all primary relationships. In much the same way that spirituality seems to enhance people's general sense of well-being, family is also capable of protecting and enriching us. Research shows that families of all types who come together regularly to celebrate milestones and holidays tend to be freer of dysfunction than those who do not. The same energy you use to play a leader in public is necessary in private too. Lou Gerstner, former chairman and CEO of IBM, makes that connection. During a keynote speech in North Carolina, he told his audience, "Whether it's in business, or public service, or in your families, distinguish yourself."

Family is a setting in which two complementary experiences can take place. We can be who we really are, and we can discover or explore new parts of ourselves. If you are a parent, some of your most difficult challenges and your greatest rewards lie in your relationship with your children. Once again, former Chrysler head Lee Iacocca provides insight. While at Chrysler, Iacocca instructed his office staff to put all telephone calls from his children through to him immediately.

By being so completely available to his kids, Iacocca sent them a powerful message about family on his list of priorities. It would appear that Iacocca's success in the corporate world was matched by his success at home with his children.

BECOMING TRULY RICH

Which leads to an interesting question, "How do we judge a successful adulthood?" A successful childhood seems easy to define. It's protected, secure, healthy, and stable. Superficially, success in adulthood is quantified in terms of money, but is this really useful or accurate? What does money really mean? What should it mean, and what can it never mean? What's the right attitude for a leader to adopt toward money?

Throughout American history, the central issue surrounding money has been getting enough of it to ensure survival. A huge segment of the population worried about putting dinner on the table. Today, part of the American population remains below the poverty level, but our most widespread pressures about money have changed. The anxiety of need has largely been replaced by the anxiety of want.

Dealing with this anxiety can take many forms. On one end of the spectrum there are people who live by the mantra "Don't worry, be happy." They just don't worry about money the way other people do. They are not wired that way. They don't worry about their spending or the "what ifs" of retirement. They don't lie awake at night. They just go for it. Period. To the other extreme, many people worry incessantly about money and not having enough of it. In fact, psychologists report that this is the biggest fear that most people have, surpassing even death or serious illness.

Do you find yourself taking one of these extreme positions or are you somewhere in between? Clearly, the answer lies in striking a balance. A little bit of caution and advanced planning can prevent most financial problems. At the same time, knowing how to free yourself from endless worry is equally important. This is one case in which the real leadership position is in the middle, at the balance point.

SUCCESSFUL LEADERSHIP IS A BALANCING ACT

In sum, balance and perspective are fundamental to personal leadership mastery: prudence balanced with freedom, work balanced with rest, career balanced with family, and material well-being balanced with spiritual awareness. Leadership in your personal life means investing in your own happiness. You wouldn't expect a large organization to run on its own, with no vision, no direction, no guidelines, and no leadership. A corporation is not a self-cleaning oven. By the same token, you cannot expect your private life to run itself either. If you don't take control of it, somebody or something else will.

TRANQUILITY OF MIND

The ideas of bringing a richness to your life experience and of taking command of the way your life is run bring us to the last leadership lesson of this chapter. You might be surprised to discover that it does not conclude with a bang. In fact, the last component is nothing other than peace and quiet.

Solitude and tranquility of mind are key to balanced and effective leadership. The time and space that you carve out of your busy life to think, to reconnect with nature, and to develop the ability to be alone with yourself should be imperatives on your priority list. Many people find sitting in a quiet space to be very difficult. Noise and the need for connection at all times are addictions and many of us have a bad case. The more electronic our society becomes, the more items we have to plug in and separate us from this simple but essential experience of quiet contemplation. Do not shortchange yourself. Do not mistake solitude for dead time or boredom. With practice, you'll be able to restore your energy and quiet everyday stress by insisting on some protected quiet time.

Above all, remember that when you put your feet on the floor in the morning, you have the power to make it a good day or a bad day. You are either going to enjoy life in the next twenty-four hours, or you are not. Remember, those hours are never going to come your way again. There are hundreds of things that can irritate, worry, or annoy you. Don't let them. Don't let the small things get you down, and if the big things get you down, take a good look to make sure they are really big.

Now that you have these strategies to strengthen your resources and apply to your personal life, you are well on your way to the private side of leadership. Without a happy and fulfilling personal life, professional success is just a job. When the many dimensions of every day are filled with challenge, commitment, love, and humor, then the possibilities are endless.

ACTION STEPS

1. Listed below are the steps you can take toward greater organization of your time. Included are some specific actions that you can take as well. Put a ✓ beside those that you believe you have mastered, and put an X beside those that you feel you need to work on. Then write out an action plan, including at least three steps that you can take toward mastering each skill.

   - Purchase an organizer or day planner.

   - Start using the organizer on a daily basis.

   - Avoid energy-draining and time-wasting activities.

   - Move the television out of your bedroom.

   - Cut down on watching television.

   - Set realistic goals. Do not overschedule yourself.

   - Avoid chaos and restore order in your life.

   - Fill up downtime (like waiting at the doctor's office or

sitting at the car wash) with activities like updating your calendar or writing to-do lists.

- Commit to creating more synergy each day (plenty of rest, nutritious diet, and exercise).

2. When you are disorganized, you will often find that the disorganization serves you in some way. For example, you may be avoiding fully stepping into your true power, because of fear. By being disorganized, you may never have the time to reach your full potential. Write down a list of potential ways in which disorganization might serve you. Then reflect on this realization, and create an action plan to clear your schedule—and the block!

3. One example of wise proactivity was illustrated by the chief executive officer who put in an exercise room at his offices. Write down three creative or innovative ideas that you could implement into your organization to create greater balance.

4. Creating intimacy and connection with family is imperative for total balance. "Father Forgets" is one of those little pieces that, dashed off in a moment of sincere feeling, strikes an echoing chord in so many people. Read and learn from "Father Forgets" by W. Livingston Larned. After reading it, reflect on your life. Where can you find more patience (don't forget to also include patience with yourself and your imperfections)? Instead of condemning, try to understand. Try to figure out why we do what we do. That's a lot more profitable and intriguing than criticism, and it breeds sympathy, tolerance, and kindness.

"Father Forgets" by W. Livingston Larned

Listen, son: I am saying this as you lie asleep, one little paw crumpled under your cheek and the blond curls stickily wet on your damp forehead. I have stolen into your room alone. Just a few minutes ago, as I sat reading my paper in the library, a stifling wave of remorse swept over me. Guiltily I came to your bedside.

There are the things I was thinking, son: I had been cross to you. I scolded you as you were dressing for school because you gave your face merely a dab with a towel. I took you to task for not cleaning your shoes. I called out angrily when you threw some of your things on the floor.

At breakfast I found fault, too. You spilled things. You gulped down your food. You put your elbows on the table. You spread butter too thick on your bread. And as you started off to play and I made for my train, you turned and waved a hand and called, "Good-bye, Daddy!" and I frowned, and said in reply, "Hold your shoulders back!"

Then it began all over again in the late afternoon. As I came up the road I spied you, down on your knees, playing marbles. There were holes in your stockings. I humiliated you before your boyfriends by marching you ahead of me to the house. Stockings were expensive—and if you had to buy them you would be more careful! Imagine that, son, imagine that from a father!

Remember, later, when I was reading in the library, how you came in timidly, with a sort of hurt look in your eyes? When I glanced up from my paper, impatient at the interruption, you hesitated at the door. "What is it you want?" I snapped.

You said nothing, but ran across in one tempestuous plunge, and threw your arms around my neck and kissed me, and your small arms tightened with an affection that God had set blooming in your heart and which even neglect could not wither. And then you were gone, pattering up the stairs.

Well, son, it was shortly afterwards that my paper slipped from my hands and a terrible sickening fear came over me. What has habit been doing to me? The habit of finding fault, of reprimanding—this was my reward to you for being a boy. It was not that I did not love you; it was that I expected too much of youth. I was measuring you by the yardstick of my own years.

And there was so much that was good and fine and true in your character. The little heart of you was as big as the dawn itself over the hills. This was shown by your spontaneous impulse to rush in and kiss me good night. Well, nothing else matters tonight, son. I have come to your bedside in the darkness, and I have knelt there, ashamed!

It is feeble atonement; I know you would not understand these things if I told them to you during your waking hours. But tomorrow, tomorrow, I'll be a real daddy! I will chum with you, and suffer when you suffer, and laugh when you laugh. I will bite my tongue when impatient words come. I'll keep saying as if it were a ritual: "He is nothing but a boy—a little boy!"

I am afraid I have visualized you as a man. Yet as I see you now, son, crumpled and weary in your cot, I see that you are still a baby. Yesterday you were in your mother's arms, your head on her shoulder. I have asked too much, son, too much.

Ask questions instead of giving direct orders.

—Dale Carnegie

CHAPTER 17

Leadership in the New Workplace

Everyone who was ever a guest of Theodore Roosevelt was astonished at the range and diversity of his knowledge. Whether his visitor was a cowboy or a Rough Rider, a New York politician or a diplomat, Roosevelt knew what to say. And how was it done? The answer was simple. Whenever Roosevelt expected a visitor, he sat up late the night before, reading up on the subject in which he knew his guest was particularly interested.

For Roosevelt knew, as all leadership masters know, that the royal road to a person's heart is to talk about the things that he or she treasures most.

Talking in terms of the other person's interest pays off for both parties. Howard Z. Herzig, a leader in the field of employee communications, has always followed this principle. When asked what reward he got from it, Mr. Herzig responded that he not only received a different reward from each person but that in general the reward had been an enlargement of his life each time he spoke to someone.

HONORING DIVERSITY

Today's leadership masters must get along with everyone, not necessarily as a best friend, but certainly to the degree that race, national origin, religion, generation, or personal lifestyle choices do not intrude. The chairman of a large manufacturing company puts this principle in perspective. "Eighty to 85 percent of the people entering the workforce in the twenty-first century will be minorities, women, or immigrants," he says. "This is not some distant point in the future; we're there right now. So, unless you want to avail yourself of only 15 percent of the talent out there, you had better get comfortable with diversity starting now."

Historically, ignorance has always been at the root of intolerance. Here is the flip side of that sad fact: The best way to gain respect for another culture or any form of diversity is to educate yourself about it. The late Arthur Ashe certainly had abundant talent as a tennis player, but that's not what led him to choose the game as a career. "I knew there was a lot of travel involved," Ashe once said. "That's really what I was looking forward to. I wanted to visit all those places. I wanted to see the things I'd only read about in the pages of *National Geographic.* I welcomed the opportunity to learn about them."

Exposure to anything new can evoke very different attitudes in different people. We may feel self-satisfied and even haughty about who we are as individuals and about the culture we come from. We may look down at people who have another sort of background. Maybe they're not as technically sophisticated, as well educated, or as physically healthy as we are. That is one way of looking at it. Another is to say, "Yes, their present circumstances are different from mine. They may have come from a rich theological or cultural heritage from which I can learn. They may have seen things I've never seen. They may know something I don't know."

For a leadership master the second viewpoint is the only approach.

Today, nations right beside each other can have totally different cultures and so can people who live next door. These differences must be acknowledged, respected, and responded to. After leading a very diverse workforce for a number of years, a computer executive offers some excellent advice: Try to avoid making comparisons. Try not to say anything that sounds like "Around here we do things this way." People feel very insulted if you suggest that their way of doing things is somehow inferior, whether you're talking about their home or their home country.

Put Yourself in Another's Shoes

Practically speaking, the first step toward living comfortably with diversity is a very simple one. Put yourself in the other person's place. No matter what their differences, we're all living, breathing human beings and our similarities are actually a lot more pronounced than our differences. Look for those things we all have in common. We all have pressures at home. We all want to succeed, and we all want to be treated with the same dignity, respect, and understanding.

Empathy, or seeing the world through another's eyes, is something a leader needs to accomplish on a daily basis. People have always wanted to be treated as individuals, but today they acknowledge their individuality in many new ways. It is not just a matter of saying "Good morning" or "Thank you" anymore. A lot of ethnocentric assumptions have to be put aside, and a lot more awareness has to take their place.

In some parts of the world and within some races and religions, it's considered rude to seem too friendly or inquiring. There are people who want routine business encounters to be just that, without much small talk or questions asked or answered. It's not hostility; it's just a sense of social distance. Other cultures, of course, have very different expectations. It's considered insulting if you don't smile, say hello, and pass the time of day for a while, even if you're pressed for time. If these two viewpoints meet head-on, with neither one knowing much about the other, there will be problems. That's what happens when people haven't educated themselves about diversity so that real empathy can become possible.

Making People Feel Important

Instead of making people feel different, many successful leaders are learning how to make people feel important. This takes more than one or two gestures or compliments. It's a process that consists of many little touches, sometimes over a significant period of time.

An executive in the garment industry describes her experience with this. "Times were tough for us in the late '80s and early '90s," she said. "But our people were incredibly wonderful in helping us get through, and they come from all over the world. I like to think it's because over the years we tried to build a sense of real closeness. We recognized our differences. We found out what they mean and what they don't mean. We certainly didn't ignore them, but we also learned to look beyond them."

In this particular company, recognizing differences meant gently correcting a visiting executive when he referred to female employees as "girls." It meant counseling a young man about his fear of driving on the freeway, so that he could get to work on time. It meant learning Spanish. It meant leaving the door of the president's office open.

Years ago an insurance agency moved into a building that housed several other offices. On his first day in the new location, the president of the agency knocked on the door of the office next door to introduce himself. When a young man opened the door, the insurance agent was surprised to encounter a strong aroma of incense. Behind the young man he could see a dimly lit room hung with tapestries and exotic artwork. It looked like something from a fairy tale, but it actually was the outer office of a jewelry manufacturing and polishing business. The young man and his brother owned the business. They had recently arrived from

Lebanon and they were looking forward to pursuing their careers in a country where bombings and civil war were not a way of life.

Although the insurance man and the jewelry manufacturers had very different ideas about how their place of business should look, they became good neighbors and eventually close friends. They learned from one another, not only about their work, but also about every aspect of their lives. They learned to see each other as individuals, not as symbols or stereotypes of some alien civilization.

OUTSOURCING WORK TO FOREIGN COUNTRIES

One of the most controversial trends in American business is the transfer of manufacturing work beyond the borders of the United States. The controversy involves the possibility that American workers are being deprived of jobs, as well as the possibility that foreign workers are being exploited by very low wages. These are complex issues, but there's no doubt, in some countries around the world, that survival is very difficult. When the owner of a large American manufacturing company visited a factory in Southeast Asia, he was deeply affected by the hard work being done. The need of the workers for any job they could get was clear to him.

As it happened, the American executive had been a student of Dale Carnegie. He recalled reading a story that Carnegie told many times over the years. The story concerned James A. Farley, Franklin Roosevelt's campaign manager during the '20s and '30s. Farley made it a practice to write down, and often to remember by heart, the names of everyone he met on his travels around the country during political campaigns. This would include many hundreds of people. Then when he returned home, after weeks on the road, Farley immediately set about a task that he considered hugely important. He sent a personally signed letter to every single individual he'd encountered on the road. This of course was smart politics, but it was also a gesture that must have had immense meaning to thousands of people struggling to survive during the years of the Great Depression and Second World War. Many probably kept their letters from Jim Farley for the rest of their lives.

As he toured the Southeast Asian manufacturing plant, the American executive thought about Dale Carnegie telling that story, and before he returned to his hotel, he had obtained a list of the names and addresses of every worker at the factory. Then, back home he sent a personal letter to every one of those names. This task took several weeks. The executive couldn't even pronounce many of the names, but he knew this was something that the factory workers would never forget. He also knew that it was one of the most positive things he had ever done in his business career—not because it made a lot of money for him, but because it didn't.

As a leader you must be aware of the demographic sensitivity of today's highly charged workplace. Small gestures mean more than ever before. Returning a phone call, remembering a name, and treating people respectfully all add up to leadership mastery. Failing to take care of these things may be nothing more than simple carelessness, but it can be misinterpreted as something much more serious by people who feel vulnerable and powerless.

As a Chicago advertising executive reports, "The small but significant gestures are what separate you from the crowd. You've got to get into the habit of making people feel important and unique, especially if they don't quite feel that way themselves. You've got to say, 'Regardless of our differences, so much about us is the same. We are in this together. You're concerns are my concerns.'"

This is really nothing more than applying the Golden Rule in the workplace. Treat everyone like a colleague, don't patronize, don't condescend, and by all means don't berate.

LOW SELF-ESTEEM

Given the dramatic changes in the American workforce, why are so many managers failing to get the message? Why are some people still denied equal access to hiring and promotion? Why do lawsuits cost companies millions of dollars when these abuses come to the surface? Often the reason is low self-esteem. Not on the part of the victims, but in the people who ostensibly hold power. "Managers feel exposed," says the vice president of a large investment bank. "They think their egos are always on the line. Many of them are really very decent people. But when certain managers meet somebody who doesn't know how important they're supposed to be, they tense up. They adopt an unnatural style. They're not really gruff or blunt but they think they've got to act that way. It's overcompensating for their own sense of discomfort."

Does this cover work? It rarely does. As the bank executive explains, "People rarely respond to intimidation or manipulation, and when you're dealing with people from different cultures or backgrounds, those kinds of behaviors are magnified by the distrust that's already present. Instead of letting their negative behaviors be magnified, leaders should make an extra effort to show consideration and respect. Today you can't make easy assumptions about how your words and actions will be interpreted. You've got to take the extra step."

Another executive puts it this way, "In our own minds we've got to be prepared to forget about our titles and our incomes. We've got to strip all those things away and focus on the contribution everyone is making, regardless of their position in the organization." And that's actually a very healthy thing to do. If you can't meet people without pinning all your medals on your chest, maybe you don't deserve those medals anyway.

Successful executives are often people who have spent years acquiring and getting comfortable with power. They are men and women who have learned how to assert themselves and move to the front of the pack. But the new workplace demands learning some humility. This is true particularly for people who have made their mark a decade or so in the past. While this is a challenge, it is also an opportunity.

One executive in commercial real estate found a great way to disengage himself from his impressive title in the corporate world. "I was a company president when I was in my early thirties," he said. "I felt very important because of that. Then I'd come home and the baby would be wet and I'd be changing a diaper and it immediately brought me back and gave me perspective. My family is what really kept me in balance."

Other leaders have accomplished the same thing through sports, religious affiliations, parent associations, and school. Leadership masters do whatever it takes to see things through other people's eyes, especially if those eyes are used to looking out on a very different environment.

ACTION STEPS

1. Honoring and respecting diversity and maintaining a work environment that does so too are key to mastering leadership. List three things that you can do to further encourage diversity in your organization.

2. It is important both personally and professionally to be able to put yourself in another's shoes. Empathy is a trait that should be valued and practiced. How empathetic are you? Next time you struggle with someone, take some time after the struggle to sit quietly and imagine the situation from his or her perspective. To do this, you must totally let your own opinions and agenda go. Then write any new insights or ideas you gain from practicing this exercise.

3. Sometimes we can get lost in the might of our ego. It is important, no matter who you are, that you are able to disengage from your title or status. There is no true power in arrogance. It only alienates you from your peers and subordinates. How can you cultivate more humility in yourself? List three steps that you can take to further develop your humility.

Keep your mind open to change all the time. Welcome it.
Court it.

—Dale Carnegie

CHAPTER 18

Diversifying and Humanizing Your Organization

While sensitivity is crucial for a leader, so is a willingness to challenge people with expectations and responsibilities. For newcomers to the American economy, work is most likely a very big part of their lives. They want to be involved. They need to be engaged. They deserve to be challenged and stretched. They don't want their opinions and their talents to be ignored or patronized. A Silicon Valley software executive deals frequently with people from India and Sri Lanka. She says, "What people want is a feeling of importance. They want to make an impact. They want a sense of influence."

How can a leader bring this about with an increasingly diverse work force? Different people require different approaches, but there are certain common denominators. As the software executive explains, you've got to assess people's talents as well as how they rate their own capabilities. Then you should ask them for just a little bit more than it seems they can comfortably give. Stretching an employee's comfort zone has to be handled diplomatically, of course, but a good leader can make that kind of challenge seem flattering. Raise your own expectations just a notch and almost anyone will respond.

ENLISTING COMMUNITY INVOLVEMENT

Earlier we discussed a large corporation in the home products industry that enlisted the support of employees and community members to enhance its business. In that corporation, that same leader continued to take raising expectations to a whole new level.

He called upon those same workers from the local community to stretch themselves into areas when highly technical expertise was required. When the company needed to design a multimillion-dollar piece of new equipment, the decisions were not made exclusively by top executives and engineers. A task force was created, made up entirely of production workers. The task force did most of the research on new equipment. Task force members visited companies that could build the machine and made evaluations. Later the task force issued a recommendation about where to buy. As it happened, the selected builder was in Europe, so task force members spent time overseas consulting and being trained. Then they returned with personnel from the builder and further work was done. In the end the new equipment was largely procured, scheduled, and quality-controlled by line workers (many of whom didn't even speak the same language as the supplier). This kind of cross-cultural enterprise will inevitably become more common in years to come. The most successful companies and leaders will be those who can take advantage of it.

HUMANIZING YOUR ORGANIZATION

This leads to a principle that can be stated very clearly: Leadership masters must humanize their organizations in ways large and small. On the surface a word like *humanize* might not seem to bear on issues like profitability and stockholder return. Unless the philosophical concerns are addressed effectively, however, the financial numbers will inevitably be brought down.

Symbolic efforts can play a big role here. The big executive desk should become a thing of the past, at least for meetings or one-on-one discussions. Most high-ranking leaders now use small conference tables or an arrangement of chairs with a sofa. In meetings with customers or employees, it makes the encounter more casual and informal, and it shows respect for their time. The whole purpose of any meeting is to share ideas and viewpoints. A more relaxed setting can generate creativity and robust discussions.

ENSURING EMPLOYEES DON'T GET LOST IN THE CROWD

The chairman of a large pharmaceutical company has moved beyond symbolism. He feels that humanizing an organization is so important that he's even structured the physical plants of his companies with that in mind. "I think employees working in a single location with 10,000 other people is a recipe for disaster," he says. "It defeats all your efforts to make people feel like important and unique individuals. When you get out of your car in the morning and walk through the parking lot with an army of other employees, it's only natural to feel devalued as a human being. You think, 'If I disappeared right now, would anybody notice?'"

For the pharmaceutical company, the solution is maintaining thirty-two physical locations. One of them is large, with nineteen hundred employees, but the rest range from three to six hundred people. "As a result," says the chairman, "we have people who walk through the parking lot knowing other people's names, and working in an atmosphere like that is fun and exciting. There's a sense of shared endeavor, which is wonderful to see in any diverse workforce."

More and more companies are beginning to agree. Facilities

of four to six hundred people are replacing the gigantic physical plants. "It's not really a matter of saving money," says one executive. "The thing we feel that is really crucial is that people build relationships. When you start getting close to a thousand employees, the understanding and the empathy goes away, especially at the supervisory level. You start having to create a whole department to deal with problems that should be handled spontaneously at the individual level. And putting together a department is expensive. So, from both a humanistic and a pure cost viewpoint, it's best to keep down the number of people in any given location."

Decisions like this are vitally important, and they are not just for top managers. Today, everyone must be a leader in addressing issues of the new workplace. All of us, regardless of job title, will get further and accomplish more by respecting and understanding one another. Although this is perhaps more important now than ever before, it's hardly a new concept. Years ago Dale Carnegie applied it to people all over the world. "It's strange," he once said. "People in one country feel they're superior to everybody in a second country, but the people over there are convinced that they're the superior ones. It's a situation where both can't be right and in fact both are very wrong. Nobody's superior to anyone else in basic human terms. Leaders should make certain they understand that, and that they get that conviction across to everyone they meet."

REVISING SOME BASIC ASSUMPTIONS

As we approach the end of this session it's important to realize that some of its basic assumptions will soon have to be revised. So far, for example, we've adopted a perspective that leaders in the new workplace come from the same demographic as thirty years ago, and that the only changes have come among line workers or middle managers. That, of course, is far from the truth and it's becoming less true every day. Outstanding leaders from every race, gender, generation, and ethnicity have gained prominence in recent years. Such leaders include the late Roberto Goizueta of Coca-Cola (born in Cuba), former Secretary of State Madeleine Albright (born in Czechoslovakia), and the hugely popular Oprah Winfrey (who has been called the most influential woman in the United States). Not long after his playing days ended, Michael Jordan became part owner of a MBA team, joining one of the most elite clubs in America. All in all, the presence of these and many other widely diverse leaders is going to bring big changes.

For the new groups now taking up the reins of influence, the challenge is more complex and perhaps even more difficult than for their predecessors. Unless you're of Native American ancestry, your forebears were likely immigrants at one time or another. As leaders emerged from what were minority groups, they often felt pressure to shed their ethnic identity in keeping with their new-found positions of power. The United States was often described as the melting pot in which the true expression of Americanism was dissolving into the molten mass. The new groups of minority leaders feel no such need. Within the context of their power and responsibilities, most are determined to retain and celebrate their diverse backgrounds. It will be interesting to see how this trend changes our expectations of leaders.

As you read this chapter, you may be one of those new leaders or you may be one of the people who make new leadership possible in the changing workplace. You may just be starting out in this exciting new landscape. In any case, from top to bottom, opportunities abound.

ACTION STEPS

1. In one of the above examples of effective leadership, the owner of a company had several members of his staff research and implement systems into the organization. This tactic proved to benefit all involved. On a scale from one to ten, rate how good you are at delegating responsibilities and empowering others.

   1   2   3   4   5   6   7   8   9   10

   I delegate very little   *I delegate often*

2. Research current or past leaders who are women or belong to minorities (in race, religion, or other). Find at least two whom you regard highly, and write a short list of reasons why you respect them. Then incorporate those traits into your leadership style.

3. One CEO actually separated his company into several smaller plants to make sure his employees did not feel lost in a crowd. While taking such drastic measures may not be necessary in your organization, what small steps can you take toward making your employees feel unique, important, heard, and like contributors to the bottom line of your business? List three new action steps you can take to create a greater sense of belonging in your organization.

Bernard Shaw once remarked, "If you teach a man anything, he will never learn." Shaw was right. Learning is an active process. We learn by doing. So, if you desire to master the principles you are studying in this book, do something about them. Apply these rules at every opportunity. If you don't, you will forget them quickly. Only knowledge that is used sticks in your mind.

—Dale Carnegie

CHAPTER 19

Practical Tactics and Techniques

Leadership principles are blueprints for everyday life. Blueprints, plans, and theories are necessary, but there comes a time when the rubber meets the road. You can't get a driver's license merely by passing the written test. You have to get behind the wheel and apply your skills on the street. As a leader, you live in a results-oriented world. You need to navigate it with speed and skill.

While strategies are the blueprint, actions are the hammers and nails of building leadership mastery. If you want to build a superior organization and develop your own full potential as a leader, the tactics and techniques presented in this session can be invaluable. They consist of a set of tools you will never want to be without.

MASTERING THE DECISION-MAKING PROCESS

We will first look at decision making, one of the defining points of leadership mastery. Despite much conventional wisdom on this subject, the key to effectiveness here is not so much in making the decision as in following through on the decision you make. We are all faced with tough calls in our careers and in our personal lives, decisions with clear pluses and minuses on both sides. Sometimes there seems no better way to make a decision than by simply flipping a coin. Faced with situations like these, too many people just freeze up. A kind of mental paralysis sets in. In larger organizations, the final decision itself may even be avoided entirely and set aside for further study.

Jack Welch's Workout

Jack Welch, former CEO of General Electric, is one of the most admired corporate leaders in the world. With a Ph.D. in engineering, he is certainly a long-range thinker with a strong practical orientation. Of all the innovations Jack Welch brought to General Electric over his twenty-year tenure as CEO, the one he considers the most important was the decision-making process known as the workout. When a group of employees at any level of the company identify a problem, they meet to discuss it and arrive at a proposed solution. They then submit both a description of the problem and the suggested remedy to their supervisor. The supervisor must then give a yes or no response within twenty-four hours, with no further discussion permitted.

Welch believes that the workout technique has thoroughly transformed GE's corporate culture. It empowers people. It gets them thinking proactively about what they can accomplish. It cuts through the bureaucracy and red tape that encumbers many large organizations. After all, if the individuals who must deal with it have carefully thought through an issue, then more time on the part of the leader would unlikely be helpful.

If the proposed solution is accepted, then both morale and efficiency stand to benefit. If it is rejected, the group retains the power to revisit the problem and arrive at a better solution. From a leadership point of view, the key element in the workout process is the removal of the leader from the discussion phase. There is no need for a leader at this point because everyone has learned self-leadership. Even a few years ago this would have seemed inconceivable in many organizations, yet it has proven its worth in one of the most successful companies on the planet. In the opinion of Jack Welch, it is literally worth millions and even billions of dollars.

As a leader, what can you learn from GE's workout process? Whether or not you choose to implement it in your own organization, it can tell you something about the benefits of team involvement, decisiveness, and follow-through. The truth is that the real challenge of a decision begins only after the decision has been made.

CLEARLY ARTICULATE EXPECTATIONS

Our second tactic would seem to be pure common sense. Ignoring it causes breakdowns in communication, frustration on the part of both leaders and team members, and lost opportunities at all levels of an organization. What is this seemingly self-evident leadership technique? Very simply, letting people know what is expected of them, and being clear about what they can expect from you.

Here is a case in point. Meg Legman owns a small chain of retail party supply stores in southern Florida. A few years ago she hired Lindsey to do all of the window and in-store displays. Meg was immediately impressed with Lindsey's initiative. She convinced Meg to clear space in the center of their largest store for a table and chairs. Lindsey wanted to fill the table with products from the store's inventory so customers would feel like they were walking right into a charmingly decorated party scene.

Meg gave Lindsey the green light and the idea was a solid hit. Lindsey changed the theme every month. Customers loved it and sales figures went up. People left the store full of ideas, and their full shopping carts reflected their enthusiasm. When Meg decided to develop a Web site for her retail chain, Lindsey seemed the ideal choice for the job. Meg wanted the Web site to be a fully interactive party consulting service. Customers would get help from the planning stages of a party all the way through the last detail. It was a great idea and Lindsey seemed perfect for making it work. That's when problems started.

Lindsey began staying late each night working on the computer graphics, researching the competition, and ironing out bugs in the concept. She even took work home. She liked the project, but at the same time she began to resent the additional responsibilities Meg gave her. Lindsey wondered if she was being taken for granted. No one new had been hired to help with her prior responsibilities and now her workload was much heavier. Tension between Lindsey and Meg began to intensify. Finally, about a month before the Web site was ready (and right after the Thanksgiving rush), Lindsey abruptly quit her job. Meg was left to scramble through the rest of the holiday season without a key employee.

Since that incident Lindsey's return has been negotiated, but it was a critical lesson for Meg. Without Lindsey and without the Web site, she lost the additional Christmas business she had banked on. A great year ended on a sour note. The lesson is this: Make sure that people know exactly what's expected of them. If those expectations change, make equally certain that the outcome is manageable. Lindsey started out with one job description, did well, and her job grew. This is usually a healthy sign of talent and hard work. The problem was that Meg and Lindsey never sat down and considered the meaning of these changes in terms of hours, qualifications, and increased responsibilities. These things were eventually addressed, but not until considerable damage had been done. Whether dealing with a new hire or a veteran employee taking on a new responsibility, a leadership master clearly needs to define responsibilities and expectations. What's more, those expectations need to be reevaluated and redefined on a regular basis.

ONLY MAKE PROMISES THAT YOU CAN KEEP

Third, be very careful about making promises. When you make one, be sure to keep it, especially if it's about salary, a bonus, or any money-related issue. A peculiar fact about human nature is that very few people ever forget a promise that has to do with money. Whether it's money loaned, money borrowed, the promise of a raise, or other commitments, you can be sure it hasn't been forgotten, even if it is never verbalized.

Avoid Ambiguity and Confusion

An important element of responsible promise-keeping is the ability to avoid ambiguity and confusion. Be very careful to make a clear distinction about what constitutes a promise and what does not.

Suppose a general contractor tells the head of one of his crews that he can probably get him his check by the next business day. This is heading into the gray area where things can easily be misunderstood. The crew chief is likely to count on the check, and if it does not arrive, frustration or anger will likely arise. This is an example of a very serious form of miscommunication. Regardless of how the employee reacts, the ultimate fault lies with the leader. He needed to be much clearer as to whether he was extending a promise, or just speculating about an outcome. Choose your words carefully, as carefully as you choose your promises.

USE HUMOR WHENEVER POSSIBLE

Tactic number four is: Use humor generously and appropriately in leadership situations. Laughter really is the shortest distance between two people, so why take the long way when the shortcut is so much more fun? This technique is best, of course, if you happen to be a genuinely funny person, but it can be used by almost everyone. Even people who are not known for being great wits have their own brand of humor they can cultivate and use to their advantage. Remember to simply be yourself. Humor can be defined in a hundred ways, and all of them equally effective.

For one manager it might be the weekly posting of a Dilbert cartoon on the bulletin board outside of his office. For another, it could be sharing an appropriate anecdote or joke at the start of a board meeting, or sending a humorous e-mail around the office.

Some years ago there was a newspaper editor in Chicago who was famous for his mischievous sense of humor. About once a month, with a very straight face, he'd assign some unsuspecting reporter a gag story that didn't really exist. Since he didn't want his editorial staff spending too much time pursuing false leads, regardless of how funny they were, he'd give the writer a contact to go along with the assignment. The reporter would dial the number of the contact, but it wouldn't be a legitimate news source. Unbeknownst to him, the editor's friend (who was in on the joke) would be at the other end of the line. After about five minutes of strange conversation, the reporter would inevitably burst into laughter, realizing he had been tricked. Much to everyone's amusement, the editor would give his latest victim a quick salute, and then get back to work. Fifteen years later, reporters who worked in that newsroom still remember it as a great place to work.

Never underestimate the power of a smile or humor. When it comes to humor, work with what you have. Your team will appreciate the atmosphere you create.

YOU CAN BE RESPECTED AND LIKED

The subject of humor brings up an old question on the philosophy of leadership: "Is it better to be liked or to be respected?" The fact is the vast majority of people in leadership roles would rather have the respect of their team over their affection. Surprisingly, this is the wrong answer. More to the point, it's even the wrong question. Framing affection and respect as an either/or dilemma is a misperception of how leadership actually works. Can you really like someone for whom you have no respect? Doesn't lack of respect generate a fair amount of anger?

There's a good chance that the separation of liking and respecting is a false distinction. Even if we accept it as valid, though, most leaders who say they want to be respected really mean that they want to be feared. This may be because they themselves are in some way frightened or uncertain. So encourage yourself to think differently on this issue. Being liked and respected are simply two dimensions of leadership mastery. Understanding and implementing this insight is tactic number five.

MASTERING ONE-ON-ONE COMMUNICATION IS KEY

Tactic number six is as important for leadership as it is for making the NBA. You need to master the game of one-on-one. Private, face-to-face conversations are supremely important when communicating and connecting with members of your team. Many leaders tend to devote much more thought and preparation to public speaking than to engaging employees in private interactions.

You may be an orator on the level of Winston Churchill, but when you are sitting alone with a member of your team, you must shift gears for a very different kind of communication, one that has its own guidelines and pitfalls.

By the very nature of the personal setting, what passes between the leader and the team member will be important. It is not for public scrutiny. It is a chance to see one another up close. If you are not exactly under a microscope, you are at least under a magnifying glass with both your strengths and your weaknesses magnified. The more pressure in a workplace environment, the more important it is for a leader to handle these encounters effectively.

In the towers of high-volume airports, traffic controllers are responsible for hundreds of flights and many thousands of lives each day. Peak performance is maintained largely through peer pressure and careful observation by the supervisor. When pressure begins to show itself in a controller's performance, the first response by the leader is a one-on-one talk with the individual. The purpose of the conversation is to relieve stress, but it is also a chance for the leader to determine whether the problem is a temporary one or one that could endanger people's lives. This calls for mastery of personal interaction. A mistake in this situation could lead to a more destructive mistake later on.

Leaks are the little holes that appear in the image of yourself that you're presenting. In this game of one-on-one you definitely want to avoid leaks. Here are a few to steer clear of in particular. Do any of these sound familiar?

- First, don't sneak a glance at your watch. You won't get away with it.

- Second, if someone who's supposedly more important walks by, do not let your eyes wander.

- Third, don't take unnecessary phone calls, and don't confuse the game of one-on-one with that other game, one-upmanship. When someone shares a problem with you, don't launch into a story of how you have solved a similar problem that was even tougher.

Mistakes are amazingly common in individual encounters, and the leadership master walks away from them unscathed.

ACTION STEPS

1. As a leader, how good are you at making a decision and keeping it? Do you vacillate too much before coming to a final conclusion? Do you second-guess yourself, and change your mind frequently? Do you avoid making decisions until the eleventh hour? What can you learn from GE's workout process? List at least two things that you can do to improve your decision-making skills.

2. Ambiguity and confusion, especially around money, can be detrimental to both you and your organization. Are you clear around the exchange of money? Do you always sign contracts before entering into work obligations? Do you sometimes make promises that you cannot keep? Write a list of ways that you could improve the clarity of your communication. Then make a point of incorporating those skills into your daily routine.

3. Instilling humor into a working environment can benefit everyone. You were provided with a couple of ideas on ways to do so in this chapter. Write out a fun or humor action plan for your organization, including at least five steps that you can implement. Give yourself permission to have fun and think outside the box. Then put your ideas into action in your organization. After all, besides uplifting spirits, laughter reaps greater enthusiasm, connection, and productivity.

You will probably find it difficult to apply these suggestions all the time. I know because I wrote the book, and yet I frequently find it difficult to apply everything I advocated. For example, when you are displeased, it is much easier to criticize and condemn than it is to try to understand the other person's viewpoint. It is frequently easier to find fault than to find praise. It is more natural to talk about what you want than to talk about what the other person wants. And so on. So, as you read this book, remember that you are not merely trying to acquire information. You are attempting to form new habits. Ah yes, you are attempting a new way of life. That will require time and persistence and daily application.

—Dale Carnegie

CHAPTER 20

Consistency, Competence, and Phone Communication

BE CONSISTENT

Our seventh leadership tactic applies to everything you do, whether it's private conversations, public presentations, or the way you sign your name. Be consistent. This is one of the things we most appreciate in another person and especially in a leader.

Consistency, of course, is not necessarily related to dullness. Being consistent does not mean you cannot be creative. Consistency is not about being on mental cruise control, or lacking in imagination or new ideas. In fact, real consistency requires full awareness and conscious effort. Leadership masters know that making that effort creates trust and motivates extra effort.

THE FOUR STAGES OF COMPETENCY

Tactic number eight is, in fact, several tactics in one. It consists of an extremely useful paradigm of performance often referred to as the four stages of competency. Although the origins of this model are not clear, it is often used to explain the stages people go through when learning a new skill.

By using this paradigm in your leadership interactions, you can meet people where they really are in their professional development. This is an important first step toward moving them to a higher level.

Unconscious Incompetence

Simply stated, there are four stages of competence in any endeavor, whether it's playing the piano or making a sales presentation. Unconscious incompetence is the lowest rung. Without making light of this (because we've all been there), the unconscious incompetent is someone who's not only unskilled but is unaware of that fact.

Ted Baxter, the anchorman character on the old *Mary Tyler Moore Show*, messed up his broadcast night after night, but he strutted through the newsroom afterward completely unaware of what had happened. Of course, what's funny on television can be disastrous in the real world.

As a leader, your challenge is to recognize when people are at this point and help them to a higher level of performance. If you think that people at this stage of competence are a tiny minority, think again. A recent study reported in *The New York Times* revealed that a huge segment of Americans consistently overrate their own abilities in a wide variety of areas. Whether they are competing obliviously on *American Idol* or overestimating their skill in English grammar, sports, or arithmetic, they really are unconscious of their own incompetence. Think about that the next time you find yourself having to evaluate the performance of your team members.

Conscious Incompetence

In the next stage, consciously incompetent individuals are still not performing well, but they're not without awareness of that fact. This is a major step forward. These individuals are honest with themselves. They are aware of their challenges, and that poses a breadth of opportunity for both themselves and the organization they are with. Being aware of their shortcomings puts them in a position to improve upon them. Of course, this is only the case when they are ready, willing, and able to do so.

Conscious Competence

Conscious competence, in turn, represents the mastery of a skill and the knowledge of your ability. A leader can rely on people on this rung of the ladder to get their jobs done successfully. Their level of performance makes them dependable, with the right mix of training, direction, and good work habits. Virtually everyone is capable of reaching this stage. Again, all that is required is a direct course of action, discipline, and a willingness and desire to succeed.

Unconscious Competence

Not everyone, however, can reach the final level of intuitive, instinctive mastery that we can call unconscious competence. Not everyone can be a Michael Jordan or a Tiger Woods. When the legendary chess master Bobby Fischer was only twelve years old, he played against some of the world's greatest players. During one game against a much more experienced opponent, Fischer made a move that seemed entirely irrational. He gave up his queen with no benefit that anyone observing the game could see. In fact, the final result of that sacrifice didn't materialize until twelve moves later in the game. Fischer himself conceded that he couldn't mentally diagram the outcome in his head in any conscious way. Intuitively, however, he felt rather than thought that this outrageous move was the correct thing to do. No computer, regardless of how much information it was designed to process, could have accomplished the same thing. His brilliance was so instinctive that his play became a completely unconscious process.

As a leader, all of the people you come in contact with will fall somewhere along the competence spectrum. It is your job to assess everyone's performance level accurately. You will quickly see just how useful this framework is in your everyday decision making. It will help you determine the kinds of responsibilities you assign, the expectations you have, and the training and development people will need. Equally important, you can apply it to yourself.

Schedule Weekly Meetings with Managers

The next point is simple: Have direct contact with all your managers or leaders at least once a week. No matter how secure people are, no matter how healthy their egos, no one likes working in a vacuum. People like having their efforts recognized. They want to know that someone notices. Put the two Super Bowl teams in an empty stadium, and they will still play good football. They would not play, however, the way they would play in front of a hundred thousand cheering fans. At least once a week there should be a one-on-one exchange between a leader and as many of the managerial staff as possible. Note, though, that it should be a two-way, reciprocal communication. Keeping the exchange as a mutual dialogue, you will gain valuable insights. Team members will receive an immense benefit knowing that there's an appreciative audience acknowledging the work that they have done.

Richard Lovett, the head of CAA, Hollywood's most powerful and profitable talent agency, when it comes to running a high morale organization, he has refined e-mail correspondence into a real art form. Not only does every single person in his agency turn on his or her computer each morning to find a new e-mail waiting, but Lovett also makes sure to send personalized messages to his key players on a regular basis.

If someone who represents the biggest stars in the entertainment world can find the time to get it done, you can too.

ALWAYS RESPOND WITHIN TWENTY-FOUR HOURS

A related tactic also applies to e-mails and, most especially, to phone calls. Always respond to these communications within twenty-four hours. The next time you get a free moment, take a look around your office. What's the most dangerous item you see for your business? Even if you have a bear trap in the corner, the most potentially destructive item in any office is the telephone. Used well, it is a gold mine for conducting business; however, used carelessly, it is a bombshell.

We use the telephone for a thousand interactions each day, ranging from ordering out a quick lunch to winning over an important customer. Phone skills, however, are a subject that very few of us think about. Even during the very first phone call ever made between Alexander Graham Bell and his assistant Thomas Watson, a portion of their conversation was misunderstood. The telephone can be dangerous because your interaction with another party is limited in several ways.

For example, you have no visual cues to go on. You have no

idea if the person on the other end is composing an e-mail, doing a crossword puzzle, or listening intently and taking notes. All you have to go on is his or her voice.

Secondly, unlike e-mail, which you can access at your own convenience, you never know when the phone is going to ring or who it is going to be. There is an element of unpredictability about it. What could be more stress-inducing than waiting for a call that you want or, for that matter, getting one that you have been dreading. In general there are interruptions, second lines blinking, and countless other small interruptions that make the phone a potentially precarious medium for communication.

Several surveys back up this startling finding. When companies were asked why they had lost someone's business, the single most cited response was that it was something that happened over the telephone.

For all of these reasons you have to practice good telephone etiquette. The cardinal rule that transcends all others is this: Always return a phone call within twenty-four hours. Like promises about money that are not kept, an unreturned phone call is another thing that people are not likely to forget. Whether they acknowledge it or not, failing to get a phone call returned is something people take very seriously. In some corporations it is considered cause for dismissal.

Perhaps you think you're too busy to get back to people within one business day. When the late George Allen was one of the most successful coaches in the National Football League, he placed calls to rival teams and timed the speed with which they returned. He found that the speed with which they returned the call very closely matched the win-loss records of the teams.

We have now covered several practical tactics and techniques for you to apply to your professional life: acknowledging the efforts of others, keeping the promises you make, using your sense of humor, focusing on the person you're talking to, keeping in regular contact, and returning phone calls in a timely way.

Some of these are easier to incorporate than others, but all of them are within your reach. Practice and commitment are all you need. By turning these practices into self-perpetuating and unconscious competent habits, you will be taking a big step toward true leadership mastery.

ACTION STEPS

1. Which of the four stages of competency are you at in the work you do?

   - Unconscious incompetent

   - Conscious incompetent

   - Conscious competent

   - Unconscious competent

2. Listed below are the practical tactics outlined in the past two chapters. Mark with a ✓ those that you believe you have already mastered, and mark with an X those that still need some attention. Then set a growth and integration plan into action.

   - Acknowledging the efforts of others

   - Keeping the promises you make

   - Using your sense of humor

   - Focusing on the person you're talking to

- Keeping in regular contact

- Returning phone calls in a timely way

3. List three things that you could do to optimize your use of the telephone in the work that you do. Then act on the insights that you receive.

When dealing with a crisis, worry can be a major mental block in getting the problem solved. Here are some fundamental facts you should know about worry. One, if you want to avoid worry, do what Sir William Osler did. Live in day-tight compartments. Don't stew about the future, just live each day until bedtime. Two, the next time trouble with a capital T backs you up in a corner, try the magic formula of Willis H. Carrier:

A. Ask yourself, "What is the worst that can possibly happen if I can't solve this problem?"

B. Prepare yourself mentally to accept the worst, if necessary.

C. Calmly try to improve upon the worst, which you've already mentally agreed to accept.

Three, remind yourself of the exorbitant price you can pay for worry in terms of your health. Those who do not know how to fight worry die young.

—Dale Carnegie

CHAPTER 21

Dealing with Crisis: The Truest Test of Leadership Mastery

In the years since John Kennedy occupied the White House, there have been many revelations about him and his administration. Some have been unflattering, yet the vast majority of

Americans still admire John Kennedy highly. Any shortcomings or indiscretions seem insignificant in comparison to his successes. In particular, one very dramatic occasion stands out. In the fall of 1962, the United States came closer than ever before to a nuclear war with the Soviet Union. During the Cuban missile crisis Kennedy showed real leadership, courage, and creative thinking under the most stressful circumstances imaginable. Today, when people think of John Kennedy, his conduct during those thirteen days in October is one of the first things they remember. This was a defining moment for Kennedy and for his administration. Along with his tragic death, this is what we most remember John Kennedy for.

CRISIS AS A LEADERSHIP OPPORTUNITY

With this in mind, we can discover an important truth about leadership and the evaluation of leaders. Very simply put, leaders are defined and judged by how they respond in a crisis. The worse the crisis is, the more important the leader's behavior becomes. Winston Churchill was considered a brilliant failure until the outbreak of World War II. Lee Iacocca was not much more than a fired auto executive until Chrysler needed someone to hold the company together. We can still view a crisis as a genuine threat that has to be addressed, but we also should realize that it's an opportunity to practice leadership mastery. It is a chance to really test yourself in the big leagues, and the purpose of this session is to help you bat a thousand.

In any crisis, whether personal or professional, there are principles that a leader should put into action. While doing so cannot guarantee that things will turn out exactly as you would like, it can guarantee that you will display real leadership mastery. Very often, your initiative to solve this crisis can certainly help you avoid similar problems in the future.

DISPLAYING CALM IN IMPENDING DISASTER

In the late '80s, there was an emergency aboard a wide-body jet-liner making a cross-country flight. The plane was somewhere over Iowa when suddenly and without warning many vital control systems failed. It was a catastrophe, pure and simple. The damage to the plane's internal system could hardly have been more severe. Flying the plane in that condition was like trying to steer a car by opening and closing the doors. An emergency landing was requested at a remote airfield in Iowa, and the plane began its perilous descent.

Owing to the pilot's almost incredible skill and performance, the plane made a crash landing with a minimal number of injuries. Although some people did lose their lives, it was a miracle that anyone survived at all. The minutes that passed between the start of the emergency and the landing could hardly have been more terrifying. Later, however, when conversations between the pilot and the control tower were broadcast on national news, it sounded like a very calm chat between two casual acquaintances. There were no raised voices, and no indication of apparent stress, anger, or fear.

This way of responding in a crisis, of course, is drilled into airline personnel throughout their training and their careers. It's a mark of professionalism, but it's also the most effective form of behavior from a practical standpoint. So, keep this first principle of crisis leadership firmly in mind. Getting excited almost never helps, and keeping calm almost always does.

Resist Emotionality

As a leader, you must train yourself to resist instinctive emotional responses. Force yourself to think positively, even if you don't believe your own reassurances. Very few situations are as bad as they seem in the moment. Even if a situation is as bad as it seems, your best course is to behave otherwise. Act as if everything is under control and chances are, it soon will be. Quietly ask yourself, "What can I do to make this situation better? How quickly should I act? Who can be of help? After I make the first move, what are the second, third, and fourth things I should do? How can I measure the effectiveness of the steps I take?"

A young woman we'll call Patty used questions like that to lead herself through the most intense crisis of her life. The day after a routine physical checkup, Patty's phone rang. Her physician wanted her back in his office as soon as possible to run some more tests. It seemed the tests already taken during routine exams suggested that Patty might have uterine cancer.

Patty was devastated by the news. A thousand dire thoughts ran through her head. And when the follow-up tests confirmed the cancer diagnosis, there was a moment when Patty totally collapsed inside. But she had always been a strong person, a person who understood the need for self-leadership in times of crisis. Soon Patty began to pull herself together.

She began asking questions of her doctor. She started doing research on her own. And gradually, the real facts of her situation began to emerge. At that stage, her illness had a 95 percent cure rate. She focused on the strong probability that, come what may, the odds of survival were strongly in her favor. Even after eighteen months of drug therapy failed to eliminate the disease, Patty concentrated on the positive aspects of her situation.

She had to undergo surgery, but at least surgery was possible and would probably be effective. "I told myself to have faith, and not to let fear destroy me," Patty said. "I put myself in the mindset that I could handle anything that life brought." Fortunately for Patty, her surgery was successful. Four years later, there was no evidence of disease. And as Patty puts it, "Every day, I face life anew."

PLACING A STOP LOSS ORDER ON STRESS

There are many ways of training yourself to react calmly. There are many techniques for diffusing the ticking bomb that a real crisis seems to represent. Dale Carnegie used to speak of putting a stop loss order on your stress. A stop loss order is what happens on Wall Street when a trader automatically sells a stock if it falls below a certain price. As a leadership master, you can learn to do the same thing with stress, pressure, and anxiety.

In a crisis, for example, ask yourself this question, "What's the worst thing that can happen?" Thankfully, most of our problems are not really of the life-and-death variety. So you may blow an account, you may miss a payment, or you may even lose your job. Will that be unpleasant? Absolutely. Is it worth the price of stress? Absolutely not.

Identifying the worst possible outcome and facing it squarely does not mean you have to accept it. It does not mean lying back and welcoming failure, especially when others depend on you to lead them toward success. It just means telling yourself, "Yes, I suppose I could accept that outcome if I really had to, but I still have no intention of letting it happen."

BREAKING CRISIS DOWN INTO MANAGEABLE INCREMENTS

By definition, a serious challenge seems overwhelming when it's confronted full force and head-on. If we stand at the foot of a mountain and look up at the top, it can seem a long way off. It can seem impossible that we'll ever get there. Perhaps, then, instead of looking at the top of the mountain, we should try looking down at the ground. We should watch ourselves take one step first, and then another. This is really the only way of avoiding the sudden paralysis that can set in when a crisis suddenly looms. As a leader, you've got to reduce the dimensions of a crisis to a manageable size. You've got to break it down into bite-size pieces for your own benefit, and for the people who depend on you.

This is such a fundamental concept that it deserves to be emphasized. How do computers perform their calculations with such incredible speed? They reduce even the most complicated problems to a series of zeros and ones, a sequence of tiny calculations that can add up to something very big. In much the same way, when planes fly across the country, the flight plan is a list of small jumps: from Chicago to Des Moines, from Des Moines to Fort Dodge, and so on, all the way to San Francisco.

The Scottish poet and novelist Robert Lewis Stevenson expressed this idea very poetically. He wrote, "Anyone can carry his burden, however hard, until nightfall. Anyone can do his work, however hard, for one day. Anyone can live sweetly, patiently, lovingly, purely until the sun goes down. And this is all that life really means."

It is possible, of course, that even after you have broken a crisis down into its component parts, you may still feel stymied. This does happen and at this point, you may have to recognize something that many people don't like to admit. Not every problem has a complete and total solution. Much as we might wish otherwise, square pegs do not fit in round holes.

SOLVING PROBLEMS ONE STEP AT A TIME

Despite the best efforts of some of the brightest minds in history, there is no way to turn lead into gold. There is no way to square the circle. There is no way to invent a perpetual motion machine.

The point is this: If you cannot see a way to solve a problem, can you at least see a way to solve part of it? Even in the direst crisis, there is almost always something proactive that you can do. Focus your attention on finding that something, and then do it, by all means. You can never tell where it might lead.

The late Peter Drucker, famed author and philosopher of

management wisdom, made a very interesting statement in this regard. "Good managers and good leaders," Drucker said, "are not problem-oriented people. They are by nature oriented toward opportunities rather than problems. Even when things seem really bleak, they focus on what can be done rather than what can't."

For these kinds of leaders, a crisis is like a crossword puzzle. There may be many words that they do not know, but even if they know only one, they realize that this is a step in the right direction. So take that small step, by all means.

Research on decision making shows that most people consider far too few options, especially when the stakes are very high. There are always positive things you can do, but seeing them is likely to take some focused attention.

Here's a rule of thumb to help with this: In a crisis, discipline yourself to make a list of no less than fifty proactive things you can do. Make no mistake, there are more than fifty if you really get yourself to think about it. Ask yourself, "What are the small changes I can make that will benefit the situation? Who are the people I can call? How can I minimize the damage? What can I do that will reveal the silver lining even within the blackest cloud?

ACTION STEPS

1. In responding to crisis, it is wise to resist emotionality. Consider a crisis situation that you find yourself in (or one that you worry may come about). Rate your anxiety level about the situation on a scale from one to ten.

   1   2   3   4   5   6   7   8   9   10

   Not worried   *Very worried*

2. Now ask yourself the following questions in response to the situation you considered in question #1: "What can I do to make this situation better? How quickly should I act?

Who can be of help? After I make the first move, what are the second, third, and fourth things I should do? How can I measure the effectiveness of the steps I take?" Once you have applied the five questions above to the situation, write out an action plan.

3. Whenever you have a crisis on your hands, you have an opportunity to be proactive and prove yourself. In a crisis, you should ideally discipline yourself to make a list of no less than fifty proactive things you can do. Make that list with the above-mentioned crisis now.

4. Now that you have proactively worked on your crisis (in questions 1, 2, and 3), make note of how you feel in response to this process. Rate yourself again on the scale from one to ten below. Has your anxiety lowered since you did the exercises above?

1   2   3   4   5   6   7   8   9   10

Not worried   *Very worried*

Here are some basic techniques in analyzing worry. One, get the facts. Remember that half the worry in the world is caused by people trying to make decisions before they have sufficient knowledge on which to base a decision. Two, after carefully weighing all the facts, come to a decision. Three, once a decision is carefully reached, act. Get busy carrying out your decision and dismiss all anxiety about the outcome. Four, when you or any of your associates are tempted to worry about a problem, write out and answer the following questions. A. What is the problem? B. What is the cause of the problem? C. What are all possible solutions? and D. What is the best solution?

—Dale Carnegie

CHAPTER 22
Mastering Crisis Management

In this chapter we will continue with proactive initiatives that leadership masters take in response to crisis. The ability to manage crisis in a calm, methodical way often distinguishes the leaders from the followers.

THE THREE PRINCIPLES OF CRISIS MANAGEMENT

The first three principles of crisis management are really statements of instruction that we touched on in the last chapter. First, be calm. Second, break it down into manageable components. And third, see if there's even a small part of the problem that you can solve. Make sure you carefully consider the problem and reflect on whether there are options you have not considered. Practicing these three principles is the foundation upon which you can delve deeper into the situation, with the assurance that you are in the optimum frame of mind.

FOCUS ON THE PAST ONLY IF IT HELPS YOU IN THE FUTURE

The next technique comes in the form of a question, one that takes you momentarily back into the past. When faced with a crisis, ask yourself if you have ever dealt with something like this before. Chances are you have. What did you learn about the nuts and bolts of solving the problem, and what did you learn about getting through the emotional turbulence that came with it? Even if the outcome was not what you had hoped for on that earlier occasion, this is a new day. That was then, and this is now. Once we learn from the past, we need not relive it unless it suits our purposes. This is what Dale Carnegie meant when he referred to living your life in day-tight compartments.

So many people waste enormous energy thinking about what happened yesterday or might happen tomorrow. In a crisis, this is energy you simply cannot afford to squander. "You and I," Dale Carnegie once wrote, "are standing this very second at the meeting place of two eternities—the past that has endured forever, and the future that is plunging on to the end of recorded time. Yet we can't possibly live in either one of those eternities, not even for one split second."

The implications of this for crisis leadership should be very clear: Use your experience to guide you in a positive direction, but realize that you're living in the here and now. The past is a resource we can draw upon, not a ghost that haunts us.

ENLIST SUPPORT

A difficult thing for any leader in a crisis is the sense of isolation that often settles in. By their very nature, leaders take responsibility upon themselves. As a result, they're sometimes reluctant to call upon others for support, especially in difficult circumstances.

If you feel that asking for help somehow undercuts your leadership, please learn to resist this tendency. Getting outside support is extremely important in a crisis, not only for making decisions, but also in dealing with the inevitable emotional stresses. If you are facing difficult times, talk to someone you trust about your thoughts and emotions.

If you keep things bottled up, they will intrude on your decision making, and your ability to lead effectively. Focusing exclusively on the problem at hand will wear you out, and it will wear out the people around you. So, find someone with whom you feel safe, and enlist his or her support. You will return to work with a clearer head and a lighter heart.

FIND TIME FOR REST AND RELAXATION

Earlier we referred to President John Kennedy's exemplary handling of the Cuban missile crisis. In recent years, there have been a number of books on that incident. They paint a clear picture of Kennedy's efforts to keep himself relaxed, even as the situation was growing darker by the minute. After hours around the conference table with his senior advisors, hours spent literally deciding the fate of the world, President Kennedy would watch a movie, play with his children, or take a nap.

While this probably required more self-discipline than anything else he could possibly have done, Kennedy knew the importance of rest and relaxation. In any crisis, force yourself to get some distance from it on a regular basis. This is by no means shirking your responsibilities. In fact, it is one of the best ways of equipping yourself to fulfill them.

AVOID BLAME AND TAKE RESPONSIBILITY

Our final point about leadership mastery in a crisis has to do with issues of blame and responsibility. Actually, the concept of blame is very easy to deal with. Simply banish all thoughts of blame from your mind, once and for all. Blame is simply wasted energy, so let it go.

As for responsibility, you are the leader. Do not assign responsibility—take it. Whatever happens on your watch is ultimately your doing. If people make mistakes, they should have been better prepared, and that is the leader's responsibility. If someone proves to be incompetent, they should never have been hired, and that is the leader's responsibility. Until you are prepared to accept responsibility for literally everything that happens under your leadership, you are not really ready to be called a leadership master.

Start accepting that responsibility right now. Your team will respect you for it, and you will respect yourself. For a real leader, there are simply no excuses.

Let's examine how this principle plays itself out in a real-world leadership situation. You may remember the incidents of the following story. It is a great example of how leadership masters should behave under stress, and there is also some insight on how they should not behave.

The spring of 1985 saw one of the most audacious management decisions in the history of American business. The Coca-Cola Company decided to change the formula of its world-famous beverage. The decision was by no means taken lightly. Huge amounts of market research showed that people wanted a sweeter flavor in a soft drink, the kind of flavor that Coke's archrival Pepsi provided.

The so-called Pepsi challenge advertising campaign, in which blindfolded consumers again and again chose Pepsi over Coke, was proving extremely effective. Finally, Coke's senior management team decided that something had to be done, and they did it. The two executives who made this decision were Roberto C. Goizueta, Coke's CEO, and Donald R. Keough, president and chief operating officer.

They were both experienced, highly respected business leaders. In the marketing crisis they faced, Goizueta and Keough concluded they had no alternative but to create a new Coke. The product was presented to the world, but what the executives didn't realize (or what they temporarily forgot) was that to the American people, Coca-Cola was more than a product. It was more than a combination of caffeine, sugar, and fizz water.

The innovation was a disaster. The public responded as if a sacred trust had been betrayed. Thousands of letters poured into Coke's Atlanta headquarters. People wrote that they would never buy another Coca-Cola. Many said they were totally confused by the change in their favorite drink. Others suspected a conspiracy of some sort. The tone of the letters ranged from sad to negative to blatantly hostile.

Within only a few weeks, the new product was becoming the laughingstock of talk show monologues and newspaper cartoons. Millions had been spent on the development of New Coke, and it wasn't bringing in a penny. "I sleep like a baby," commented CEO Goizueta. "I wake up every two hours and cry." As the pressure mounted, the company's management team realized that something had to be done.

Finally, less than three months after the new product was introduced, Coke's management held a press conference to announce a retreat. The old drink would be brought back by popular demand. At the press conference, Donald Keough spoke eloquently about the reversal. "We love any retreat that has us rushing back toward our best customers with the drink they love most," he said. "Some people will say Coca-Cola made an incomprehensible marketing

mistake. Others may say we planned the whole thing." Goizueta said, "The truth is, we are not that smart, and we're not that
dumb."

This was true leadership mastery. Instead of making excuses
or assigning blame, the Coke executive actually referred to his
love of the customer, even while acknowledging a humiliating
defeat. In fact, he used the word *love* twice. He found a way to por-
tray the whole experience as somehow gratifying and fulfilling.
The Coke management team did not blame anybody, and nobody
blamed them, either. Within a short time, Coke was more successful than ever.

In the years since the new Coke fiasco, the short-term costs of
the episode have faded, but the leadership mastery of Coke's management in dealing with their mistake remains very clear.

A POOR EXAMPLE OF LEADERSHIP MASTERY

Unfortunately for the Coca-Cola Company, that lesson was apparently lost on a more recent leader who faced another management crisis in the summer of 1999. Douglas Ivester had been
president and chief operating officer of Coca-Cola since the mid-
'90's. Shortly after assuming leadership, Ivester stood behind
the podium at an industry trade show, and made a speech that
introduced himself to the world. There was no doubt about it. He
wanted to be seen as an aggressive, take-no-prisoners manager,
and the title of his speech was "Be Different or Be Damned." This
was the general patent of the soft drink business. This was Vince
Lombardi. During his talk, Ivester even compared himself to a
wolf—ravenous, fierce, and self-sufficient.

"I want your customers," he declared. "I want your space on
the shelves. I want every single bit of beverage growth that exists
out there." Please notice that the word *love* does not occur in this
quote. There is no reference to love of the customers or the joy of
rushing toward them with the drink they love. Instead, there's a

marked prevalence of the first-person singular pronoun, the little word "I."

It is not a word that leadership masters usually emphasize, and it cannot be found anywhere in the quote from Coke executive Donald Keough. Keough, in fact, seemed to prefer the pronoun *we* (a word, by the way, that's much more compatible with leadership mastery). As it turned out, the late '90s were not a particularly good time for the Coca Cola Company under the leadership of Douglas Ivester.

In an incident in Belgium, tainted Coke made a number of schoolchildren ill. In human terms, this was a much more serious situation than the new Coke controversy. Yet Ivester did not respond with the customer-focused attention displayed by the company leaders in 1985. Instead, he determined that it was a minor problem related to carbon dioxide. He might have been correct if the whole problem had been simply a matter of chemistry, but Ivester was very mistaken with respect to the need for true leadership and communication. He did not respond publicly to the tainted Coke crisis until it had received intense negative attention all over the world. Whatever the facts of the Belgian incident, the perception of it was made worse by a leader's failure to communicate appropriately.

If this were not enough, a marketing misstep made soon afterward seemed to seal the fate of Douglas Ivester as Coca-Cola's CEO. Somehow he came up with the idea of a vending machine equipped with a thermostat that would raise the price of drinks as the weather became warmer. While the concept may have made a good skit on *Saturday Night Live*, it was without a doubt one of the least appealing business ideas of modern times. When an idea such as this comes from the leader of a bona fide American institution, it is bound to receive intense media coverage. Not surprisingly, a few months later, members of Coke's board of directors forced Douglas Ivester out of his job.

If Dale Carnegie had been present during discussions of the

thermostatic vending machine, there is no doubt what he would have said. It would not have been criticism of the idea, of course, because Carnegie was rarely negative and didn't believe criticism was productive. He may have even acknowledged that it was an interesting idea, but Dale Carnegie's whole philosophy tells us that he would have wanted a machine that lowered the price instead of raising it. It is unfortunate for Coke that Carnegie was not at those meetings, because his idea would have made millions.

ACTION STEPS

1. As listed in the opening of this chapter, the first three principles of crisis management are the following clear statements of instruction:

   - Be calm.

   - Break the crisis down into manageable parts.

   - See if there's even a small part of the problem that you can solve, and if there are options that you have not considered.

   Write a description of a difficult situation that you are facing in some area of your life (the more difficult the situation, the better). Then describe the approach that you are currently taking to deal with the problem. After reviewing the above three principles, list at least three other options that you may apply to solving the problem (perhaps even options that you once seriously considered, but then rejected).

2. Dale Carnegie suggested that you take the following steps to break your worry habit before it breaks you. Place a ✓ beside those suggestions that you believe you have clearly

mastered, and put an X by those that you need to continue to work on. Then focus on putting these steps into action the next time worry begins to fester within you.

- Crowd worry out of your mind by keeping busy. Plenty of action is one of the best therapies ever devised for curing worry.

- Don't fuss about trifles. Don't permit little things, the mere termites of life, to ruin your happiness.

- Use the law of averages to outlaw your worries. Ask yourself, "What are the odds against this thing happening at all?"

- Cooperate with the inevitable. If you know what circumstances are beyond your power to change or revise, say to yourself, "It is so—it cannot be otherwise."

- Put a stop loss order on your worries. Decide just how much anxiety a thing may be worth, and refuse to give it any more.

- Let the past bury the past—don't saw sawdust.

- Reflect on your life and take note of what you spend time worrying about. Write these items down on a list, and then in your imagination, take each of them to its worst-case scenario. Make a point of using the myriad tools that we have given you to work through each worry. Keep working on them until the anxiety fades. Remember, whatever you do, take action. Nothing is more debilitating than inaction and paralysis.

Remember that other people may be totally wrong, but they don't think so. Don't condemn them. Any fool can do that. Try to understand them. Only wise, tolerant, exceptional people even try to do that.

There is a reason why the others think and act as they do. Ferret out that reason—and you have the key to his actions, perhaps to his personality.

Try honestly to put yourself in his place. If you say to yourself, "How would I feel, how would I react if I were in his shoes?" you will save yourself time and irritation. Becoming interested in the cause, we are less likely to dislike the effect. In addition, you will sharply increase your skill in human relationships.

—Dale Carnegie

CHAPTER 23

Building a Firm Foundation for an Unpredictable Future

In this chapter, we'll look back at some of the concepts that we covered, and also at the Dale Carnegie principles that are their foundation. We will then look ahead to how you can put these concepts to use in your own daily life, not just in theory but also in response to real-world leadership challenges.

THE EVOLUTION OF LEADERSHIP
IN A CHANGING WORLD

We will begin by turning our attention to the immense changes that have taken place over the years. Until recently, America has enjoyed economic prosperity. The good times that attended the dawn of the new millennium have been compared to the postwar boom of the '50s, but there is at least one very significant difference. In the '50s, Americans really believed that the good times would never end. We were the conquerors of the world. We had it all figured out. We believed that we were not only different from everybody else, but a lot better.

Needless to say, like today, some surprises were in store. Eventually, the postwar boom and the American economy went bust in a very big way. The oil crisis in the '70s was perhaps the first sign of this, followed by a general perception that America might no longer be able to compete in the expanding global marketplace. Japan suddenly seemed to own the future. In everything from cars to television sets, the Japanese took our own products, made them better, and sold them back to us.

Then a few other unexpected developments took place. American high technology moved out of California garages and onto the world marketplace. The leading edge of the most profound economic revolution since the invention of the steam engine was firmly centered in the United States and nowhere else. What's more, the cold war geopolitical environment that had dominated the world for forty years suddenly evaporated. This, too, seemed to come out of nowhere, and suddenly the whole meaning of leadership was fundamentally altered. The image of the leader as a stern-faced military commander abruptly gave way. We no longer needed someone to lead us into battle. We needed leaders who could deal with change, work effectively with a diverse population and workforce, and model in themselves the ethical, emotional, and spiritual qualities expected of them.

All these are immense changes, but what can we learn from them? How can we understand them in a comprehensive way? What is the thread that links the sudden economic rise of one country, the sudden fall of another, and the even more sudden disappearance of others still? In a world of so many quick scene changes, how can we grasp the overall plot?

DEALING WITH AN UNPREDICTABLE FUTURE

Actually, there is one link among the unpredictable changes of recent decades: their unpredictability. During the boom years of the American economy in the '50s, there was a sense that things were going to just keep getting better and better. The future looked like a straight path toward an Americanized world, with GM cars in the garage, GE refrigerators in the kitchen, and RCA televisions in the living room.

On a larger scale, futurists of the '50s predicted space travel and cities beneath the sea, where new pioneers would feed themselves on algae grown on vast undersea farms. Rocket ships were the coming thing. Computers were not unknown in the era of Sputnik, but they were seen as cumbersome curiosities. At best, an offshoot of the robot would soon be doing all of our work for us. Virtually no one foresaw what was really going to happen. The world's best and the brightest minds were totally blindsided by the information revolution. They were also surprised by the war in Vietnam, the runaway inflation, the gasoline shortages of the '70s, the taking of the American hostages in Iran, the fall of Communism, and the collapse of the Asian stock markets.

LEADERSHIP MASTERS ARE FLEXIBLE AND PRINCIPLED

The point here is not to disparage anyone's ability to see what's coming down the track. Nobody knows what the future holds.

Whatever the outcome, it will probably be very different from what anyone expects. As a leader, therefore, you should be both flexible and principled. You should be prepared to adjust to sudden change, but at your inner core, certain beliefs, values, and behaviors must remain steadfast no matter in what directions the winds are heading or how hard they blow.

DALE CARNEGIE'S PRINCIPLES ARE UNIVERSAL

To his great credit, Dale Carnegie seems to have been just this sort of leader in both his life and his work. Did Mr. Carnegie anticipate all the changes that took place in his lifetime? No, he did not. He did something, however, even more important. He created a set of timeless principles that hold true regardless of the exigencies of the moment. As things have turned out, they are uniquely suited to our high-stress, fast-moving, uncertain world of today.

First and foremost, Dale Carnegie counsels us to look at life from other people's perspectives. This is an absolutely essential quality in a leader, yet it seems to become more difficult as a leader's authority grows.

In ancient Rome, when a victorious military commander returned to a celebration in his honor, a slave was assigned to stand behind him as the general's chariot paraded him through the streets. The slave had a very important assignment. Every few moments he was to softly whisper into the hero's ear, "Remember, you are mortal"—just like any other man. Today there are surely people in leadership positions who could use that advice. But leadership masters work every day to see life and themselves through the eyes of others.

Viewing Things from Another's Point of View

The late Sam Walton hired full-time employees whose only job was to stand near the front door of a Wal-Mart store, greet customers, and point them in the right direction. In fact, Sam Walton often performed that job himself in his frequent visits to stores around the country. Why did he do this? Why did he pay other people to do it? It wasn't just his down-home hospitality. He was wise enough to see his own business as his customers saw it. He knew they were stepping into a huge, brightly lit store, perhaps for the first time. He knew they needed guidance. He knew they would appreciate a store that provided it, and they would probably come back.

Looking at things from the other person's point of view doesn't happen by itself. It is a quality of leadership mastery that most of us have to develop with focused attention. It means asking a lot of questions and listening closely to the answers. The questions aren't complicated, but they have to be asked again and again, at work, at home, and with friends and acquaintances. What life experiences do other people bring to this interaction with you? What are they trying to achieve? What are they trying to avoid? What will it take for them to feel that this encounter has been a success?

The answers to these questions will be different every time, but they are all part of learning to see things from other people's points of view. They show that you are making a sincere effort to learn what someone else is really looking for, and as a leader, you are helping them to get it. As Dale Carnegie said, "If you can learn what other people's problems are and help them to solve those problems, the world is your oyster."

Genuine Appreciation and Interest Are Key

If getting in touch with another person's perspective is largely a matter of listening, motivating them to positive action is closely linked to what you say and how you behave. This is where leadership masters understand the importance of genuine appreciation, recognition, and praise.

Whether you are dealing with the president of a Fortune 500

company or a clerk in the supermarket, everyone wants to be told they are doing a first-rate job. Everyone wants to be told that they are smart and capable, and that their efforts are being recognized. A little bit of appreciation at just the right moment is often all it takes to transform an indifferent, disengaged team member into a star player.

"Why is it," Dale Carnegie once asked, "that we're so often inclined to voice criticism rather than praise? We should use praise at the slightest sign of improvement. That's what inspires the other fellow to keep on improving." It is not complicated at all, but for some reason, many people find it hard to distribute even well-deserved praise. A case in point is an East Coast insurance executive who, by his own admission, always found it difficult to offer positive feedback. As he describes it, "I was never able to tell someone 'You know, I really appreciate you.' I was never able to say, 'Thank you for all you've done, thank you for all the extra time you've put in. Thank you, because what you're doing is terrific.'"

After years of holding back, the insurance executive finally recognized the responsibility of a leader to give praise. In part, he learned it from his own boss. "He's a remarkable person," says the executive. "He'll tell you when he thinks something isn't going well, but at the same time he finds a way to include something positive. It's so reassuring to hear that."

ACTION STEPS

1. We have no way of knowing what the future holds. A leadership master is flexible and quick to respond, whatever the situation may be. On a scale from one to ten, rate your flexibility (one being not very flexible, and ten being very malleable and flexible).

1	2	3	4	5	6	7	8	9	10

Inflexible   *Very flexible*

2. When engaging with others, it is important to be open to the skills that they bring to the table. Focus on something that currently requires some initiative within your organization. Focus your attention on those involved and ask yourself the following questions: What life experiences do other people bring to this interaction? What are they trying to achieve? What are they trying to avoid? What will it take for them to feel that this encounter has been a success?

3. Make a list of the team players with whom you are involved in your organization. Write three qualities that each member possesses. These would be positive traits, assets to the decision-making process. Provide specific evidence of each quality or trait. Share your observances with each member as encouragement and an indication of your trust in them.

In his book How to Turn People into Gold, *Kenneth M.*
Goode says, "Stop a minute to contrast your keen interest
in your own affairs with your mild concern about anything
else. Realize, then, that everybody else in the world feels
exactly the same way! Then, along with Lincoln and
Roosevelt, you will have grasped the only solid foundation
for interpersonal relationships, namely, that success in
dealing with people depends on a sympathetic grasp of the
other person's viewpoint."

—Dale Carnegie

CHAPTER 24

Putting It All Together

In today's workplace, too many leaders fall back on money
as their primary expression of appreciation. Salary, bonuses,
benefits, and perks are the kinds of rewards most people in
authority think about. There is no denying that money is important. In truth, though, money is only one of the things people
look for when they go to work every morning. Whether they realize it or not, self-respect and the respect of others are every bit
as important.

A LITTLE RECOGNITION GOES A LONG WAY

The CEO of a large glassware manufacturer has found a way to
serve this need for recognition and appreciation, and it doesn't involve any financial payoffs. Instead, it's simply a matter of taking

employees' suggestions seriously. At one time, this CEO recalls, he used to solicit employee feedback in a halfhearted way. A few suggestion boxes were installed in the corners of plants and offices, and that was about it. Mostly the boxes just gathered dust. Occasionally a small cash reward would be given to someone who came up with a good idea, but it might take six months before that actually happened. This created as much resentment as appreciation, because anyone who didn't get the money would be angry at whoever did.

Today the suggestion boxes are gone, along with the whole approach they represented. There's still an employee suggestion program, by all means, but there's no money awarded. Instead, recognition comes in the form of an employee-of-the-week award with a picture-taking ceremony and a public expression of appreciation. That acknowledgment makes the program work. The new suggestion system is a huge success. If employees miss the money, the CEO reports no indication of it.

Team members participate for a variety of reasons. Clearly they want to improve the quality of their working lives, and their ideas are a step in that direction. Just as certainly, however, they take part because they want the self-respect and the public recognition that comes with submitting a good idea. The CEO himself was surprised by the strength of this motivation, but not anymore. "People care about making things better, and they want to know that I care about their efforts to achieve that. People may work in order to earn money, but they go the extra mile because of recognition, praise, and the intangibles. All you have to do is say thank you, and it's amazing what happens."

As a leader, how you show appreciation is much less important than doing it consistently, again and again and again. Always reward excellence, or even a sincere attempt at excellence. Encourage highly motivated participation wherever you find it, whether it's in an employee's presentation or your daughter's play on the soccer field. Reward effort, not just results.

HARNESSING ENTHUSIASM

It is also all about harnessing the mighty power of enthusiasm, another element of leadership that Dale Carnegie was quick to identify. As a salesman himself, and later as a teacher of sales techniques, he swayed minds and hearts by the power of sheer enthusiasm. It is infectious, and it makes people respond. This is true in the classroom, in the corporate boardroom, and on the campaign trail. As a business leader, if you are not enthusiastic about the direction of a company, do not expect your colleagues to feel any differently. As a parent, if you do not show enthusiasm about your children's progress in school, do not be surprised if progress grinds to a halt. As an individual, if you are not deeply enthusiastic about the direction your life has taken, you should certainly consider going in a new direction that will lead you to feel differently.

On the subject of enthusiasm, one thing must be perfectly clear: Loudness does not equal enthusiasm, nor does pounding on the table or jumping up and down and acting like a child. While that is acting enthusiastic, it is not being enthusiastic. People will very quickly see through the act because it is obvious. It is fake! It doesn't fool anyone. In fact, it usually does more harm than good. Enthusiasm has to come from inside. No real leader should confuse authentic enthusiasm with mere hype.

When Neil Armstrong stepped out onto the surface of the moon in 1969, the whole world was waiting for what he would say. Speculation had been rampant for months about the words that would surely go down in history. As it turned out, his voice was quiet and composed, but his great enthusiasm still showed through. He did not need to yell and scream, or dance a little jig. "One small step for man, one giant leap for mankind" said it all. While the words were few, the enthusiasm was overwhelmingly present in Armstrong's thoughtful words.

EAGERNESS AND ASSURANCE

True enthusiasm is made up of two elements: eagerness and assurance. Neither of those elements has to be strident or overbearing. Leaders know how to convey both excitement and a sense of self-control. If you can bring both eagerness and assurance into your voice, your enthusiasm will come across. You will have it, and others will know you have it.

Dale Carnegie once asked the president of the New York Central Railroad how he chose his associates, the people on whose abilities the company would rise or fall. His response might surprise some. "The difference in actual ability between those who succeed and those who fail is neither wide nor striking," he said. "But if two people are equally matched, the one who is enthusiastic will have the scales tipped in his favor. What's more, an enthusiastic person with second-rate talent will often outstrip someone with greater gifts."

In short, enthusiasm is as important as high ability and hard work. We all know brilliant people who accomplish nothing. We all know people who work hard but get nowhere. Those who work hard, love their work, and convey a positive attitude and enthusiasm, however, will go places.

ACQUIRING ENTHUSIASM IN YOUR LIFE

As an aspiring leadership master, how can you bring this quality into your own life? Dale Carnegie explained it this way: "Acquiring enthusiasm is a matter of believing in yourself and in what you're doing. Once you feel this way, tell someone about it. Let them know what interests you and what you're so excited about."

Keep in mind, also, that enthusiasm is easiest to attain when you can take real pleasure in your life. There should be things that you genuinely look forward to. When you wake up in the morning, you can always think about something good that will happen that day. It does not have to be anything earthshaking. Maybe it's some part of your job you really enjoy. Perhaps you anticipate meeting a friend after work, an hour on the squash court, or an afternoon browse in a bookstore.

Whatever the pleasing event might be, what is really important is this: Life should be enjoyable and interesting. Build this conviction into everything you do. When you do, watch the impact it has on the people around you. They will grow more productive and eager to respond to your leadership. Passion is always more powerful than cold ideas, and real enthusiasm is irresistible and contagious.

DEALING WITH NEGATIVE PEOPLE

We have spoken about the willingness to praise and the power of enthusiasm on the part of a leader. There is no denying, however, that a leader will sometimes encounter people who lack these qualities. As important as it is to be positive, we must also know how to deal with negative people. Sometimes their negativity may be justified. Leaders make mistakes. Leaders are subjected to criticism. Leaders, after all, are only human.

There are two fundamental facts about mistakes. First, everyone makes them. Second, no one likes to admit them. We all bristle when the accusing finger of responsibility is pointed our way. Nobody wants to be on the receiving end of a complaint, especially if it is justified. Leaders, however, balance the fact that nobody is perfect with the fact that no one likes criticism. It is not always easy to keep both those balls in the air, but it is not impossible, either. With a little practice, this juggling act can be mastered by anyone.

Admit Your Mistakes

The first step is to create an environment in which no one is above constructive criticism. Leaders who place themselves on a pedestal will sooner or later be laid low. So, spread the word again and again that shortcomings, including your own, are a natural part of life. In other words, admit your mistakes. Setting this example is very important for a leader. You can't expect others to do what you will not undertake on your own. If you really fumble the ball, live with it. Be prepared to say, "This is entirely my fault. I take full responsibility and I'll do everything in my power to see that it doesn't happen again."

It is also very important for a leader to make these statements as quickly as possible. Admit your mistakes before anyone else has a chance to point them out. It is all right to laugh about them, but not in an attempt to minimize their impact. Be very clear about that. If you can master the art of admitting fault, you will find that something very surprising begins to happen. People will rush to reassure you. Everyone will bend over backward to make you feel better. Superiors and subordinates alike will hurry to lift some of the weight from your shoulders. This is just how human psychology operates.

A very dramatic example of this occurred in the 1957 Kentucky Derby. Willie Shoemaker, one of the greatest jockeys of all time, was riding the favorite. With a little more than a quarter mile to go, Shoemaker was leading the race, but then he made an almost incredible mistake. He misjudged the location of the finish line and stood up in his stirrups several hundred yards too early. It was an error that not even a first-time rider would be likely to make, let alone an experienced professional riding a top-rated horse.

Needless to say, Shoemaker lost the race. A few moments later, the owner of the horse confronted Willie Shoemaker outside of the edge of the track. "What happened?" the owner asked. Shoemaker looked him in the eye. "I blew it," he said. "There's nothing else I can say." Reflecting on this, years later, the owner of the losing horse was able to laugh about the incident. "When he admitted his mistake, I just put my arm around his shoulder and told him to forget about it. But I'll tell you this—if he tried to come up with some excuse, I would have punched him in the nose."

In practical terms, the lesson here is very plain: Leaders always behave like leaders, whether they win the race or lose it because of their own mistakes. Leadership mastery ultimately is less a matter of what you do than what you are. What you do may vary from day to day, but what you are should remain steadfast and unchanging.

Dale Carnegie spoke very clearly about this. "Patience, perseverance, and consistency will accomplish more in this world than the most brilliant transitory moment. Remember that when things go wrong. Of course, discouragement will come at times, and the important thing is to surmount it. If you can do that, the world is yours."

The rules set down here are not mere theories or guesswork. They are tried-and-true formulas that will lead you on a path toward your own sense of deep fulfillment and true empowerment. They do not call for years of thought or self-scrutiny. All that is required of you is honesty and a genuine desire to become your own unique style of leadership master. Give yourself permission to be creative. Think as far as you can out of the box, and above all, honor yourself for your individuality and the commitment you have made toward bettering yourself. Dale Carnegie once said, "These techniques work like magic. Incredible as it sounds, I have seen them literally revolutionize the lives of many thousands of people, and they can do the same for you."

ACTION STEPS

1. Do you have a currently employee recognition plan in place in your organization? If so, how can you improve upon it? If not, take the necessary action steps to create one.

2. We all have to deal with negative people during both our personal and professional lives. Effective leaders can point out one's mistakes in a positive and proactive way,

while at the same time being clear and constructive. How might you improve your interactions with negative people in your organization? As both a leader and a model, how might you improve your own reaction to mistakes that you make?

3. Leadership mastery action plan: As a review of the work that you have already done in previous action step segments of the book, and as an exercise in gaining further insights, write your answers to each question below, and act on them as soon as possible. You hold the keys to your future as a powerful and prolific leader!

   1. Who are the individuals with whom you need to communicate more effectively?

   2. How can motivation and mentoring enhance your effectiveness as a leader? How can you help others to make their best effort—and how can you bring out the best in yourself? Is there an area in your life that could benefit from your having a mentor, or do you know someone for whom you could play that role?

   3. How can you develop the talents of those who look to you for leadership? How can you use hard work to maximize your own talents—and to strengthen areas in which natural talent may be lacking?

   4. How comfortable do you feel with risk in your own life? Are there areas in which a more adventurous approach might benefit you and your organization? Or, upon reflection, do you feel you may be a bit too ready to stretch prudence to the breaking point?

5. The book discusses two different types of leadership: inspirational and organizational. In which leadership style are you the stronger? How can you improve on both?

6. Identify any areas of difficulty that you might have in balancing professional achievements with your personal responsibilities and fulfillment.

7. Where can you put the leadership mastery tools that you have learned into use right now? What relationships can they benefit? What projects can they further? By putting these tools into action, whom can you help?

8. Are you satisfied with how you have handled crises in the past? What would you have done differently? What lessons can you draw that will assist you in discovering the opportunity lying hidden in even the most dire situations?

About the Author

Dale Carnegie was born in 1888 in Missouri. He wrote his now-renowned book *How to Win Friends and Influence People* in 1936—a milestone that cemented the rapid spread of his core values across the United States. During the 1950s, the foundations of Dale Carnegie Training® as it exists today began to take form. Dale Carnegie himself passed away soon after in 1955, leaving his legacy and set of core principles to be disseminated for decades to come.

Today, Dale Carnegie Training partners with middle market and large corporations, as well as organizations, to produce measurable business results by improving the performance of employees with emphasis on leadership, sales, team member engagement, customer service, presentations, process improvement, and other essential management skills. Recently identified by *The Wall Street Journal* as one of the top twenty-five high-performing franchises, the Dale Carnegie Training programs are available in more than twenty-five languages throughout the United States and in more than eighty countries. Dale Carnegie includes as its clients four hundred of the Fortune 500 companies. Approximately seven million people have experienced Dale Carnegie Training.

For more information, please visit www.dalecarnegie.com.

ABOUT DALE CARNEGIE TRAINING®

Dale Carnegie partners with middle market and large corporations, as well as organizations, to produce measurable business results by improving the performance of employees with emphasis on:

- leadership
- sales
- customer service
- presentations
- team member engagement
- process improvement

Recently identified by *The Wall Street Journal* as one of the top 25 high-performing franchises, Dale Carnegie Training programs are available in more than 25 languages throughout the entire United States and in more than 80 countries.

Dale Carnegie's corporate specialists work with individuals, groups and organizations to design solutions that unleash your employees' potential, enabling your organization to reach the next level of performance. Dale Carnegie Training offers public courses, seminars and workshops, as well as in-house customized training, corporate assessments, online reinforcement and one-on-one coaching.

For more information, please visit www.dalecarnegie.com.